*The Best of*

# The Passionate Speaker

*A Collection of Essays*
*from the Newsletter for Speakers*

By
**Mike Landrum**

First published by Dog Ear Publishing
4010 W. 86th Street, Ste H
Indianapolis, IN 46268
www.dogearpublishing.net

ISBN: 978-159858-732-6

This book is printed on acid-free paper.

Printed in the United States of America

# Table of Contents

# Introduction

Public speaking has become an increasingly important activity in the modern world. Each day, hundreds of thousands of presentations are made in business, government, education, religion, and the arts. Speaking is an essential tool for marketing, politics, advertising, selling, preaching, teaching, entertaining, informing, motivating, and inspiring. The ability to speak well is a meta-skill required by leaders in nearly every field of human endeavor.

When the founders of the United States of America placed the freedom of speech first on the Bill of Rights, they were recognizing its primal place in the life of society. Subtract that freedom, and you take away personal expression of all types in all media. Even mute action and strictly graphic presentations are legally protected by this constitutional amendment.

To be a speaker, then, is to express oneself to the world, and to be a passionate speaker is to express your most meaningful thoughts and feelings. When I began this newsletter for speakers, I thought in narrower terms than these. My audience, I thought, would be those who actually mounted the podium to speak as part of their work or pleasure. As the project grew, however, so did the subject. I found connections to the speaker's art in many unexpected places—from the Museum of Modern Art to the plains of Africa. I have been gratified to find support from readers who are not public speakers and never intend to be. It seems that my net has brought me a second, richer catch than the one I cast it for.

Many of these essays pivot on personal events and stories about me. It may seem a simple act of egoism, and that is a charge I have heard from some quarters. But these stories and anecdotes serve a larger purpose, I hope. The art of the speaker is a personal one, and often requires delving into one's personal history and experience. The audience has a right to expect a whole human being, speaking from a full, rich life. This material can lend weight to the speaker's insights and help the audience know the evolution of the speaker's point of view.

I believe that speakers, like actors, writers, and artists, have a mission to communicate as well as possible; that means including the personal and specific along with the universal and the general. We can best achieve rapport and "buy-in" by telling stories, making metaphors, and drawing parallels from the whole span of our experience.

A speech is a relationship, a dialogue between one and many, a complex communication of facts, feelings, needs, and desires. When a speech works well, when the relationship is a good match and the circuit is closed successfully, everyone leaves a little better for the experience.

Although *The Passionate Speaker* sometimes focuses on the techniques and methods of speaking, its wider aim is to stimulate and provoke the creative imagination of readers and followers of the speaker's art. I believe that speakers are in the vanguard of the human search for meaning, and it is with that view that I offer these essays. I owe a great debt of gratitude to Toastmasters, the National Speakers Association, and the many wonderful members of those organizations who have helped and supported me.

# 1 — Stories

"Tell me a story!" my six-year-old daughter says to me.

It's bedtime, but she doesn't want to listen to that hard fact; she wants to hear a story. We humans love a good story; that's why language was developed. Each of us has a story to tell—at least one, and often many. It is through our stories that we understand ourselves, each other, and the world.

I heard a speaker recently who wanted to inspire his audience toward greater creativity. His energy and passion were palpable, and his enthusiasm was total. "Let your ideas soar!" he implored. "Trust your heart, your intuition, your higher self! Freedom takes courage!" He went on in this vein for a while, grand words and phrases echoing like thunder in his speech—and we in the audience sat unmoved. Then he told us a story.

The British governors of India from the 19th century and well into the 20th had levied a tax on salt. They forbade the people to make salt in their traditional fashion by trapping sea water in shallow pools and letting it evaporate. In 1930, a skinny little man dressed only in a loincloth and sandals took his walking stick and led his people on a 79 day march to the sea to make salt in defiance of the British law. This simple act of civil disobedience was the opening of Mahatma Gandhi's non-violent campaign that finally won independence for India.

We listeners leaned forward, moved. We got the point.

Concepts and abstractions are often difficult to grasp. Like a whale on the beach, they can become an obstacle, indigestible and useless. A story is more like a tasty little fish in a frying pan—specific, edible, and meaningful—a much more entertaining way to nourish your audience while getting your point across.

As speakers, it is difficult, if not impossible, to arouse the interest and passion of an audience without a story. The Ten Commandments would be only a dry list of authoritarian abstractions if it weren't for the story behind them. Every great religion has succeeded because of stories that made people believe and conquer. Joseph Campbell wrote in his great work, *The Hero with a Thousand Faces*, "Our myths define us, and give us a point of reference in this uncertain life."

I do not mean to say that your speech should be nothing but stories. That might leave your audience wishing for "more matter and less art." Certainly, the "matter" matters. But our situation is rather like that of the dramatist in Samuel Johnson's couplet:

> "The drama's laws the drama's patrons give,
> For we that live to please, must please to live."

Give your patrons the pleasure they deserve. Audiences are all wishing for a story. Give them one, and they will follow you into almost any argument you care to put forward. You could even persuade a child to sleep.

## 2 — "Giving" the Speech

As we approach the holiday season we find certain words coming up more frequently. "Give," "deliver," and "present" have strong associations for us as speakers as well. "Present" has two pronunciations, but both apply to those who step forward to speak. We have to be fully present to present. We "give" a speech, "delivering" it to our listeners.

Too often, we speakers lose sight of the giving part of our trade. We step onto the platform with the idea that we are the important people in the room. After all, we have the microphone and the lectern and the lights are on us, as is the attention (we hope) of everyone else. It's easy to forget that we are bringing a gift.

What's it like for you when you bring a holiday gift to a loved one? Are you hoping for appreciation? Maybe you'd like a round of applause or even a standing ovation? That would seem a bit churlish and self-serving, don't you think? It's more likely that you are hoping your loved one likes it, that they find it useful, beautiful, needed, or wanted  You probably watch them closely while they open it and get a certain thrill when they understand at last what it is and how it will fit into their life. If it is truly a gift, the giver's attention is on the receiver, isn't it? Otherwise it's something else—like a bribe for attention.

Perhaps we need to ask ourselves if we are actually "giving" our speeches. Is our attention on the audience? Are we looking to see if they have really received it? Are we really *delivering* our message, or are we sort of floating it out like a paper airplane and leaving the effort of catching it to the audience? When we make eye contact, is it for the purpose of finding out how the audience is doing—or how *we* are doing?

When I am in an audience, I always appreciate generous speakers—speakers who look me in the eye, pause to see their words land, and watch closely to see their words' effect. I like to listen to people who take the time and trouble to give me a present—or a presentation.

### Something to Ponder

"The harder you chase something, the faster you go—and the less you're able to let life meet life. If you're having difficulty coming up with new ideas, slow down. ... Creativity exists in the present moment. You can't find it anywhere else."

—Natalie Goldberg

The human voice is the most sensitive instrument of communication. It can convey subtle nuances of thought with an almost limitless variety of inflection, pitch, tone, timbre, color, volume, and clarity. . . . We run out of words to describe the qualities of human speech. Our voices reflect our souls, perhaps more than any other single human trait can. Being so sensitive, our voices also betray our weaknesses and fears; sometimes we use our voices to hide.

Maya Angelou, the great American writer and poet, tells one of the most moving stories about hiding vocally. When she was a child, she was molested by a man, and when she named him, the man was taken out and killed. Convinced that speaking his name had caused the man's death, little Maya became mute. She was sent to her grandmother in the rural South to recover, and her grandmother read Dickens to her with great power and emphasis: "It... was... the... best... of... times,... it... was... the... worst... of... times...."

Maya Angelou has become one of the most distinguished and distinctive voices in American letters, and she credits her remarkable grandmother with teaching her the restorative power of language and the healing power of the human voice. Voices like Ms. Angelou's are rare treasures; but most of us could improve our vocal range and power simply by learning the necessary techniques.

With proper coaching and a few simple exercises, most people can improve their vocal range, power, stamina, diction and quality.

The voice is the richest, most versatile communication tool we possess. It is also the most overlooked and under-rated, in terms of the attention we give it when thinking of our presentation skills. Most people take their voices entirely for granted. Ninety percent of Americans have never taken a course in singing, breathing, enunciation or any other subject that would improve their vocal skills. That's a shame, because just a little time and effort can bring valuable benefits.

## Improving the Voice Starts with the Breath

The foundation of all vocal work is the breath. We each begin our lives breathing correctly—if you have the opportunity to watch a baby, you will notice that it is belly breathing. Most adults return to this natural way of breathing when they're asleep, but in our waking lives, our breath becomes constricted by the tensions of poor posture and the anxieties of modern life. In waking, our breath is often kept higher, in the chest, causing the need to raise our shoulders to inhale  and greatly reducing our air capacity.

To create a more pleasant, powerful and effective vocal instrument, we must start with our breathing. When we were born, we breathed naturally from our diaphragms. A newborn can scream at the top of its lungs all night long and not wear out its voice. Why? Its voice comes out unimpeded because vocally, it is completely relaxed. Its voice is a force of nature and the center of power is in its abdomen. Most adults are vocally shot by half time of the basketball game. What's happened? Tension has brought the center of vocal power up to the neck and upper chest.

Would you like to have a clear, resonant voice again, with the power to fill an auditorium and the stamina to speak as long and as often as necessary? Then you have to rid yourself of that vocal tension high in the chest and shoulders, and drop your power center back where it belongs in the lower abdomen. This means learning some good habits, or more precisely, un-learning some bad ones. Begin with a full stretch and a conscious relaxation exercise to rid tension from all parts of the body. It's strange, but true, that the whole body is the vocal instrument, and even tension in the feet affects the voice. Your first task is to breathe correctly, from your natural power center. If you lie on your back on the floor, supporting your head with a book or small cushion, you will probably find yourself breathing correctly. Your belly should rise with each inhale, and fall with each exhale, quite naturally. You need to be fully relaxed for this to occur spontaneously. If it doesn't seem to work that way for you, it means your bad habits are well established, and you'll have to pay more conscious attention to your breathing for awhile.

Imagine that your torso is a rectangular elastic box. With each inhale you inflate the box on all six of its sides – front, back, left, right, shoulders and pelvic floor. When you lie on your back, the front seems the most elastic. Can you also fill the spaces around your kidneys, between your ribs and pelvic bone with air? Even your pelvic floor  expands slightly with each breath. Your chest and shoulders, restricted by all those bones, do not expand so easily, do they? If you let your chest and shoulders stay quiet, your breath will descend into your lower abdomen. Now you are breathing from your power center – low.

Relaxation is the key to great vocal performance. Take care not to overdo these exercises. Hyperventilation is not our goal here. Just take nice, easy breaths – exploring deep and shallow ones, light and strong, from a center below your navel. Once you've been able to establish abdominal or "belly-breathing" on your back, you must bring it to work on your feet. Keep the sensation of breathing low as you work with the exercises on the next page.

## Exercises for the Voice

*(There are countless exercises for relaxing, strengthening and focusing the voice. These are only a sampling for you to experiment with. For best results, consult a coach or voice specialist who can work on your specific vocal problems. If you have difficulty locating such a coach in your area, contact the Voice and Speech Trainers Association, at www.VASTA.org )*

Stretch. Big muscles first, arms, back and legs – reaching for ceiling, bending sideways, flopping over and hanging from the waist, arms dangling, knees relaxed. Then roll up back from pelvis, one vertebrae at a time.

Shoulders, neck and face. Jam shoulders up to ears and hold for ten seconds, then drop them with a sigh. Roll head gently around in a circle, releasing tension in neck. Alternately squeeze and stretch muscles in face. Shake it out and let face go rubbery.

Yawn. Yawning is the best way to relax and open your larynx. Experiment with yawns vertically and horizontally. Shake out face and blow out lips between exercises. Vocalize a sigh as you release tension.

Sigh. Good release for tension anywhere in the body. Breathe it out on a sigh.

Breathe deep into your torso. Let a sound appear on the next exhale: "Fa-fa-fa-fa" very quiet. Repeat three times allowing yourself to breathe in a normal rhythm. Jaw is loose and dropped, posture erect and centered. Breath originates below the belly button.

Now vocalize: "Ha-hum-ah" gently. Repeat and hold the "Hum" a little longer. Find the vibrations in your sinuses.

Sing! Singing, even bad singing is useful exercise for developing the voice.

Call "He-e-e-e-y-y-y-y" as though to a friend some distance away.

Articulators - "P - T - K" unvoiced, using only the lips and tongue. Then, voiced, they become "Buh – Duh – Guh." Repeat with a brisk rhythm.

Here's a lyric from Gilbert and Sullivan that will test your articulation as well as your breath control. See if you can do it comfortably in a single breath.

> "I am the very model of a modern major general,
> I've information vegetable, animal, and mineral.
> I know the Kings of England, and I quote the fights historical
> From Marathon to Waterloo, in order categorical."

## Something to Ponder

"Not only is there a right to be happy, there is a duty to be happy. So much sadness exists in the world that we are all under obligation to contribute as much joy as lies within our powers."

—John S. Bonnell

# 4 — Passion

*"Passion is universal humanity.*
*Without it religion, history,*
*romance and art would be useless."*
—Honoré de Balzac

What are our passions, and why should we speak of them? Passion does not flow naturally and easily in our culture, I'm afraid. I was raised in a small town in the Midwest by middle-class parents whose values centered on good manners and honesty. I can't recall the word "passion" being used at the dinner table—or if it was, it was in reference to something unseemly and out of control, like sex.

Our education system is set up to discourage passion. Strong feelings of any sort usually mean trouble. "Just learn the facts and stay in line" might have been the motto of school in my formative years, and I was a most obedient student. That I was a "good boy" was always a point of pride for me until I grew up and realized that I had been "good" instead of "great" or "awesome." When I was a child, being good was nice and safe. Nothing frightened me more than the idea of being "bad." I had a lot to learn – even about being good.

When I was in my twenties, living in New York, I took a photography class from a grand lady of the camera named Lisette Model. She had been an expatriate in Paris in the 1920's and knew Picasso, Gertrude Stein, Hemingway, and other famous members of the "Lost Generation." She became a passionate photographer of passionate people. Lisette took one look at my carefully composed and mostly inert photographs, and said to me, "I see your trouble. You want to take good pictures."

"Yes, I do," I said defensively.

"I suggest you take the film out of your camera for the next week. Carry the camera around your neck but don't look through it. Whenever you have a feeling, any feeling, press the shutter."

A week was not nearly enough time. I was in my late twenties then, and I left her class a bit stung and bewildered. I had very few feelings, I found, and they were covered by a thick shell of good manners, the desire to be liked, and an ever-present fear of offending anyone. I was passionless. There were plenty of others like me, of course. Lisette drew and quartered our prints with her unerring eye.

"This picture wants to make me think there is a feeling behind it," she would say of some colorful banality. "But it's a trick, like advertising. It's a lie. You can lie at anything, you know. You can lie while scrambling eggs."

Lisette's lessons have stayed with me verbatim for thirty years now. I have worked, suffered, and finally bloomed; and now when I find feelings—any feelings—they press a button somewhere deep inside, where I acknowledge them gratefully. Of course, I am still discovering feelings and passions. I hope to go on doing so as long as I live.

When I decided to call this publication *The Passionate Speaker*, it was with Lisette's lessons in mind; our passions act as a sign post or a compass bearing, pointing us to our real destinations. When we speak passionately, we are telling something true about ourselves. It is "reason on fire," as the saying goes, and we recognize it as an authentic expression of our humanity.

## Vocal Skill Exercise

Do you know a poem by heart? Why not learn another? Spend an hour or two reading poetry aloud, alone or with someone. Relish the words as you utter them. Listen to the resonance they set thrumming in your body, mind, and soul. Here's the opening stanza from a favorite of mine:

from "Fern Hill"
by Dylan Thomas

Now as I was young and easy under the apple boughs
About the lilting house and happy as the grass was green,
  The night above the dingle starry,
    Time let me hail and climb
   Golden in the heydays of his eyes,
And honoured among wagons I was prince of the apple towns
And once below a time I lordly had the trees and leaves
    Trail with daisies and barley
   Down the rivers of the windfall light.

## Something to Ponder

"An idealist is one who, on noticing that a rose smells better than a cabbage, concludes that it will also make better soup."

          —H. L. Mencken

## 5 — Begin with the End

In my dog-eared copy of Steven Covey's book *The Seven Habits of Highly Effective People* (an eighth habit would be consulting this terrific book!), one of my favorite chapters is titled "Begin with the End in Mind." Covey uses this habit to discuss the importance of working from a Principle Center and developing personal and organizational mission statements. "Begin with the End" is also an important practical suggestion for someone who is sitting down to write a speech.

It seems to me that the first thing to think about when writing a speech is how it will end. What do you want the audience to take away with them? What is the "bottom line," the summation, the single most important thing you have to tell them? If the meeting planner rushed up to you at the last minute and said you had only thirty seconds, rather than the thirty minutes you had prepared, what would you say in that short time?

Vincent van Gogh once said that in his art he was working to paint "everything that was essential and nothing that was obvious." That's a good motto for a speaker considering what to say with the final moments of a speech: What's essential? What is the point of the information? What do you want to persuade the audience to do?

Once you have that decision firmly in hand, you can begin to elaborate and decorate with examples, anecdotes, quotes, humorous stories, and so on. In other words, the second thing to write after the ending is the middle. Here is the place to take the essence of what you want to say and develop it as a composer might make variations on a theme. Turn your idea in different directions and look at other facets and ramifications. Plumb the depths of your subject and explore as many of the funny, mundane, and profound aspects of your idea as occur to you.

Finally, pick out the best four of these stories, quotes, examples, and metaphors you've come up with. Of these four, choose the one with the strongest impact, and let that become your opening—phrase it in such a way that it becomes a "grabber." The remaining three stories, quotes, statistics, or examples then become, with the addition of smooth transitions, the body of your speech. See if this simple method shortens your preparation time for your next speech and frees you up for a bit more rehearsal!

## Vocal Skill Exercise

This sentence contains one of the more difficult tests of skill in articulation. Did you find it? It comes up in a single word. It happens when the consonants s-t-s come together, as in the word "tests" above. The careless will pronounce the word "tess" with perhaps a slightly elongated "ss" sound. Ideally, we should be able to hear all

three consonants, with the final "ts" coming as a unit—
as in the words "tse-tse fly". Here are some other words
to practice with:

> Insists
> Wrists
> Crusts
> Lists
> Masts
> Boosts

Practice with these until the "t" succeeds in asserting
itself between the "ss"es.

## Something to Ponder

"Ultimately, man should not ask what the meaning of
his life is, but rather must recognize that it is he who is
asked. In a word, each man is questioned by life; and he
can only answer to life by answering for his own life; to
life he can only respond by being responsible."
—Viktor E. Frankl

My grandfather used to say "the joy is in the doing." He was a man of many talents who worked all his life for DuPont as a facilities engineer—the only engineer on the DuPont payroll without a college degree. My grandfather had a genius for the mechanical; he could make almost anything with his hands and his tools. He loved his work, especially when there was a problem to be solved.

Once, a railroad tank car, destined for the du Pont plant, had been left on the wrong siding by mistake, three miles from the place it was supposed to be. There was no engine available to move it, and it was important that it be in the right location the next day. Grandfather struggled with the problem. Could he find an engine? Could it be towed by a truck? He consulted every other du Pont engineer available, men with doctorates. No solution arose. Finally, he fell exhausted into bed and dreamed that there was a slight grade in the rail bed and that if he only released the brakes on the tank car, it would roll the three miles by gravity alone. Next morning, he tried and found that it worked just as his dream had foretold.

This story became one of the legends of the dinner table at our house. The story was potent with meaning, though the moral was never that clear to me. Was it about the power of dreams? The vastness of the human mind? Or was the hand of God involved here? Now that I am older,

I think it was about the nature of grandfather's joy in having a difficult problem to solve: a joy so rich and absorbing that it followed him into his sleep. There, the entire library of his being was opened to him, and he found a page in the volume of his instinct that gave him the answer.

It pleased him mightily that intellect and knowledge had been useless, that he had not solved the question with his mind, but with his relationship to nature. It had not been a topographical map that told him about the incline of the ground; he had known it in his body, instinctively, the way a bird or fish knows when and in which direction to migrate. He was thrilled to discover such a knowing in himself.

This is worth remembering when choosing a topic to speak on. All the learning and knowledge we have scavenged together like academic magpies may not carry us as far as the knowing given us by nature. Isn't it exciting when a good speaker expresses a thought that seems to come from a chamber deep beneath the mind? We experience such an event as an insight or an "Aha!" That's the sort of gem we are sifting all this rhetorical sand to find, isn't it?

Give a little priority to that search. In your research for your next presentation, set aside your books and articles for a while and consult your intuition. Perhaps you can provide your audience with some new insight that scholars have overlooked. We listeners will be grateful to you,

for such natural utterances always find their way effortlessly, by a kind of gravity, into our hearts and lives.
They are the thoughts that make us aware of ourselves as
humans being human beings. "Being" trumps "knowing" every time, and "understanding" is often just the
consolation prize, isn't it? Sometimes the most creative
thing to do is to simply . . . take a nap.

### Something to Ponder

"Men stumble over the truth from time to time,
but most pick themselves up and hurry off as if nothing
happened."

—Sir Winston Churchill

# 7 — Performance Alignment

*"How we feel about ourselves governs our performance."*

Brian Tracy, speaker, author

I have read some books on speaking that cast aspersions at the idea of performing. One must not perform, these writers say, because that is phony, not an authentic way to behave. Actors perform. Speakers are not actors, and performance therefore is forbidden to them; they must be real.

I disagree.

A good performance will be, by the act itself, an authentic one, an expression of the true self. What is the human personality if it is not the performance of the self, never mind human—my dog has an infectious personality, and she goes into a regular song and dance of marvelous self-display at each glad reunion. Is she being inauthentic?

Perhaps these detractors of performing are being led astray by *poor performing*. It's likely that they consider the *desire* to perform the cause of people overdoing the job and making a hash of it. I can agree that it is preferable to see no performance rather than an ugly one, but telling humans to stop performing is as useless as telling us to jump into the air and not come down again.

Better advice is to learn to align your performance. What does that mean? A poor, unaligned performance is one that is diffuse and scattered. The speaker, actor, dancer, politician—whatever flavor of poor performer you choose—is trying to not perform. He or she is, nevertheless, in a constant state of self-analysis and judgment, watching him- or herself with critical eyes and ears to make sure he or she is being authentic. Because this is a left-brain activity, a person constantly analyzing is never living in the present but is always in the immediate past, agonizing over the gesture, the utterance that just occurred.

This sort of untrusting, self-conscious hoo-hah goes on all the time in every audience art. The problem is alignment: The performer cannot control the overwhelming number of disparate variables: inflection, timing, pitch, expression, meaning, action, vocal variety, eye contact, staging, visuals, interpretation, hair positioning, whether the audience can see the sweat on the performer's face.

It's like trying to hold twenty ping pong balls with your bare hands. It can't be done. You need a net, or your hat, or webbed fingers.

You'd have no problem holding onto twenty paper cups, though, would you? Why? Because they can be stacked, aligned. You could probably manage fifty, or even a hundred. Alignment lets you multiply your power, because you only have to pick up the bottom cup, and the others will go right along. If a speaker develops good skills such as excellent eye contact, crisp diction, a resonant voice that carries to the back of the room, and so on, the only thing left to consider is the purpose of this particular performance.

For the speaker with alignment, the bottom cup is always the understanding, and acceptance, of the fact that a good performance requires skill. Once you have developed this skill, you can start to load the performance with meaning and purpose. The advantage of alignment is that you need concentrate on only a single intention—the intention of the performance—rather than keeping track of all the little subintentions.

Performing is a set of skills; authenticity is a state of being. One does not preclude the other—to be skill-less is not to be more authentic. Rather, the opposite is true: Performing your skills well will allow you to express more of your being more authentically.

### Something to Ponder

"Gratitude unlocks the fullness of life. It turns what we have into enough, and more. It turns denial into acceptance, chaos to order, confusion to clarity. It can turn a meal into a feast, a house into a home, a stranger into a friend. Gratitude makes sense of our past, brings peace for today, and creates a vision for tomorrow."
—Melody Beattie

Years ago, I splurged on a tour of Kenya's game parks, a sort of "carpeted safari," from one expensive hotel to another. At Tsavo, a huge preserve in the savanna, south of Nairobi, our hotel was built next to a water hole where the animals gathered to drink. We tourists could sit, safe and comfortable, on our shaded private balconies, with our vodka tonics, and watch the lower orders of the animal world as they struggled to survive.

Toward evening, I became fascinated by a herd of impala—about twenty females, the harem of a single, magnificently crowned male—as they approached the water hole to drink. They were being harassed by four hyenas preventing them from getting to the water. The impala formed a circle in the tall grass, each individual facing out watchfully.

The hyenas surrounded them, and from time to time, one or another would make a feint at the herd, obviously trying to separate one of the antelope from the group so it could be attacked and devoured. The impala would immediately gather at that point in the circle to bring more sharp hooves to bear on the attacker, who would then break off the charge.

The impala would then restore the circle and make a sort of coughing bark to one another to signal that the circle was still intact. The hyenas also "talked" to one another with their ghastly cackles.

It was a stalemate. The hyenas could not break up the herd, but the impala could not get to the water. The sun went down, and in the moonless night, the standoff continued in nearly total darkness. I sat listening, fascinated, as if it were a radio drama.

Time and again, I could hear the sounds: a hyena charging through the grass, the warning bark of an impala followed by a sudden scurry of the herd to defend, then a stillness as all parties listened intently, then reassuring impala coughs from around the circle that all was still well, and the frustrated cackles from the hyenas. This went on for hours. Soon, the other tourists had retreated behind sliding glass doors to their civilized beds, but I sat on, transfixed.

The tension was palpable and relentless. I found myself deeply moved that these antelope lived their lives at this degree of focus and attention, suffering the fear of mortal danger, for hours, just to get a drink of water. When I went to bed after midnight, the standoff was still unresolved. The next morning, there were no carcasses on the ground, so I assume that the herd eventually managed to out-wait their attackers and succeed in slaking their thirst.

What possible relevance does this have for speakers? I thought of this scene recently when wondering about the origins of stage fright. Surely we humans, in the dim beginnings of our development as a species, must have encountered similar situations to the one those antelope faced.

There's safety in numbers. That was certainly the reason we primates developed powerful social bonds. Language surely evolved from something like the alert-coughs of the antelope herd. The danger of leaving the group, standing apart and alone, in front of a crowd of potential "hyenas," might be the origin of stage fright.

At some remote point in our evolution as social animals, an individual stepped forward voluntarily, in spite of this fear, and claimed the role of leader. This dramatic moment echoes in every speech and presentation, every act of politics or war, every performance, religious cele-bration, and work of art. Through courage in overcoming that knot of dread in the pit of the stomach, we humans have crossed the gulf between the brutal grassland of Africa and the balcony of that hotel.

How can it help us as speakers to become aware of these ancient patterns? In two ways, I think: First, we can rest from resisting the fear as old as humanity itself, which will always be there at the moment we rise to speak. To make ourselves wrong with the thought "I should not be feeling afraid," is both useless and destructive. Second, as speakers, our task is to lead. That anxiety that keeps the mass of followers following highlights the courage of those who rise and step forward to master their fear.

There is a bonus for the brave: The anxiety fades quickly and is soon replaced by the nourishing encouragement of our audiences.

## A Vocal Skill Exercise

The key to a full, rich, resonant voice is relaxation. This is why singing in a warm bath is such a pleasurable experience for many people. As we relax, our authentic voices emerge, and in a tiled bathroom, we can hear them, clear, full, and round. I recommend singing, especially in the shower or tub, as an exercise for speakers.

When relaxing, my old friend and master voice coach Dennis Carlo Patella suggests, you should start with the big muscle groups—the back, arms, and legs—and then move to smaller groups. Give everything a vigorous shake.

A good yawn does wonders for relaxing the throat. A vigorous stretching and contracting of the face will relax those muscles. Breathe deeply into your lower abdomen and, keeping a loose, relaxed throat and face, try singing "Ahh" up and down a scale that seems comfortable to you. The idea is to let the voice flow freely, unimpeded by tension. Then, launch into your favorite songs and let the rafters ring!

### Something to Ponder

"The most beautiful thing we can experience is the mysterious. It is the source of all true art and all science. He to whom this emotion is a stranger, who can no longer pause to wonder and stand rapt in awe, is as good as dead: his eyes are closed."

—Albert Einstein

In the mid-1960s, a high school student—poor, black, living in the slums in Washington, DC—had gotten a job as a busboy in a big hotel. In the course of his work each night, he noticed all the food scraps that were thrown away. He thought, "There's a waste." He investigated and discovered that there was a market for grease, so he got the other busboys together and offered them two dollars a night if, when they scraped the dishes, they would toss the meat scraps into a separate garbage can that he provided. Soon, he was selling fifty pounds of leftover steak fat a day. He went around to the other hotels and made the same deal with those busboys, and by and by, he was a major supplier. He had to leave the busboy job.

He looked down the line and saw that all this animal fat was being processed into lipstick. (I'm sorry if this is news to you; don't let it spoil your next kiss.) Our young entrepreneur went to the lipstick manufacturer and worked out a deal to supply the animal fat and take his payment in the form of tubes of lipstick. He even got to pick the colors. Suddenly, he was in the cosmetics business. He found out what colors the girls in his neighborhood liked, and then he hired them to sell his brand of lipstick. Nobody in the '60s was targeting poor black girls for cosmetics, so he had a monopoly on his niche market.

He wasn't finished. While he was spending all this time on the loading dock collecting fat, he noticed something else the hotels were throwing away: soap—all those little personal-sized soap bars that are unwrapped, used once, and pitched out. So he went to the maids and offered them a few bucks to put all the discarded soap into another one of his garbage cans. He took the soap to his cosmetics manufacturer, and they simply ground it into powder for use in public restrooms. By the time he got out of college, this creative fellow* was worth a great deal of money, had a thriving business, and was a great role model for others.

We live in the information age; "Knowledge is power," people say. I have to disagree. Knowledge is not power. Power comes to people who have the imagination to put their knowledge to work. "Imagination is more important than knowledge," Einstein said. Imagination plus action equals creativity, and creativity is power. After the age of information will come the age of creativity. It's not what you know; it's what you *do* with what you know that counts.

So, speakers, if you think your audience is coming to hear you just because you know something, think again.

---

* Back in the 1970s, I was hired to host a video for a government agency. During that job, I interviewed the subject of the story you just read. He was an impressive and dynamic young man, and through the years, I have remembered his story—but, I'm embarrassed to admit, I've forgotten his name. If anyone can tell me, I would be most grateful and publish it in a future issue.

Knowledge is way overrated. There's very little new knowledge in the world anyway, and what there *is,* was published in the newspaper at least a day before you are scheduled to stand up and deliver a speech.

Quit depending on what you know. Get creative. Turn your facts into a story. Use words that inspire images in the mind. Write something radical when you're writing your next speech. Make five mistakes on purpose. Look in your wastebasket—maybe you've thrown away something imaginative, something useful. . . something powerful.

## Sharpen Your Vocal Skills

The diphthong [ai], which is the long i sound that we hear in fine, hide, and bright, is sometimes a problem for speakers who have grown sloppy in their diction. A combination of the sounds ah and ee, it needs a proper balance between the two.

In the southern states, this diphthong is often drawled into a mostly "ah" sound. In some urban areas, it becomes quite nasal, and ee dominates. Here are a few practice sentences. Work with them, paying attention to where in the mouth these sounds are formed, and let them flow easily and lightly into balance. Proper pronunciation will compel you open your mouth wide—a habit many "lip lazy" speakers have lost entirely.

Clyde tried twice to climb up the fire escape.
Irene was delighted by the sight of the brightly lighted sign.
The light was so bright that it blinded his eyes.

## Something to Ponder

"Champions aren't made in the gym. Champions are made from something they have deep inside them—a desire, a dream, a vision. They have to have last-minute stamina, they have to be a little faster, they have to have the skill and the will, but the will must be stronger than the skill."

—Muhammed Ali

*"If we begin with certainty, we shall end with doubt;*
*but if we are content to begin with doubt,*
*then we shall end in certainty."*

—Constantin Stanislavski

When I was a young actor arriving in New York to begin my career at last, I found a handwritten index card on the bulletin board at Actors Equity. It read: "Never threaten an actor's insecurity." We actors are filled with doubt, it's true. We cannot get away from the overwhelming question, "Am I any good? Do I have talent?" Even the great British actor Sir Laurence Olivier lived in mortal dread of being revealed a fraud. Most people doubt. Most people are uncomfortable with their doubt, because we would prefer things nice and safe and certain.

I had a director once who, rehearsing a play, would say to us that our performances were becoming too safe and certain. We had created for ourselves a comfortable plan and a routine that we could count on. For example, Julia would always enter with a certain tempo and slap me on the word "bastard," and so on. We were all cooperating beautifully with each other, and as a result, the play was becoming a static, juiceless exercise. So the director would tell us that it was time for us to "kill our babies."

We would have to ruthlessly abandon all the perfect line readings and favorite bits of business we had developed.

He wanted to reintroduce the element of doubt into our playing. Only then would we have something real and unexpected to react against. Only then would the spontaneity return to our acting, and the audience be able to experience a living play.

Even when a performance goes well, there is doubt. Again, Olivier provides the classic example of this. In the 1930s, he was playing Hamlet at the Old Vic, and one night, his performance soared to artistic heights beyond anything even he had ever achieved. After the final curtain, his friends in the audience rushed backstage to congratulate him, and to their amazement, they found him in a towering fury, breaking furniture and trashing his dressing room.

"But, Larry," they said, trying to calm him down, "you were magnificent!"

"Yes!" Olivier shouted back to them, "it was a brilliant performance, but I don't know why!"

I have a theory about why Olivier's brilliant performance of Hamlet caused him such frustration. Of all the roles in literature, Hamlet is the most ambiguous. He is the very personification of doubt. The puzzle of the centuries for actors, scholars, and audiences has been, "Why doesn't Hamlet kill the king?"

The most obvious answer is because he doubts. He doubts the ghost, his sanity, his mother, the evidence, his courage, the will of God . . . everything. That is why it is considered the most modern and quintessentially human of all Shakespeare's plays. When Laurence Olivier became Hamlet, he spent those hours on the stage in that very state of doubt. Of course he could not "know" why the performance was brilliant; the performance was about the impossibility of knowing.

We yearn for certainty . . . for something solid, concrete, and secure that we can depend on. But in this life, taxes notwithstanding, there is only one thing we know we can count on for certain: death. (Perhaps doubt itself is another thing that will always be present for us.) Hope and doubt describe a continuum, so that a person cannot profess the one without acknowledging the other. It was a hope/doubt about the finality of death that inspired the pyramids.

Now I am older (which is not to say old), and wiser (which, alas, is not to say wise, either), so I see doubt's essential purpose now. Doubt is the harbinger of change; it has been the first sting of the spur to every human revolution—political, scientific, artistic, cultural, personal, and religious—and therefore, doubt is essential. If we were somehow able to conquer and banish doubt from the human heart, all progress, all creativity—indeed, all certainty—would vanish with it.

Robert T. Weston, Unitarian Universalist minister, wrote, "Cherish your doubts, for doubt is the attendant of truth. Doubt is the key to the door of knowledge; it is the servant of discovery . . . Therefore, let us not fear doubt, but let us rejoice in its help: it is to the wise as a staff to the blind . . . "

It's important to keep a little supply of doubt handy when you speak of those things you believe most sincerely. There is an odd, contrary reaction in most of us that creates doubt in our hearts when we are faced with expressions of absolute certainty so that if a salesman or politician or religious fanatic makes some sweeping statement of certainty, a small, insistent voice in us says, "perhaps not."

Confidence in a speaker is a great asset, but the complete absence of doubt is the definition of hubris. To remember and respect those human doubts will preserve your humility—and allow your listeners to come closer to your faith.

## Speaker's Tip

Relaxing in public is a problem that faces many speakers who find themselves seated on a dais, eating hotel food as they wait to take their turns at the lectern. There is no opportunity to stretch, warm up the voice, or run in place to get some blood flowing to the brain again. What to do? Here are some suggestions:

First, behind the cover of a napkin, yawn. Give it a good, gratifying stretch of the mouth and throat—there are few exercises so liberating to the muscles of the voice as a wide-open yawn. Second, put your notes away (you should be prepared by this time) and, assuming this is not a heavy event like a memorial, engage your neighbors in some friendly banter. The ideal would be to provoke some hearty laughter, if you can do so appropriately. Finally, put some attention on your posture. Sit up as tall as you can, lengthening and relaxing your spine. Let your shoulders drop, and carry yourself lightly and loosely as you rise to speak. Bring this light, easy style to your opening remarks, and you will have begun well, adopting an easy, natural, conversational style that shows a relaxed, alert mind.

## 11 — A Sailing Lesson

*"Everything human is pathetic.*
*The secret source of Humor itself is not joy but sorrow.*
*There is no humor in heaven."*
—Mark Twain

There we were, in our brand-new, twenty-foot sailboat, ripping across Raritan Bay at a terrifying speed. I had a death grip on the tiller with the right hand and on the rope that controls the mainsail with the left. My girl-friend, Gabe, was sitting in the fetal position, holding on for dear life. Our sailboat was tilted over at a 45-degree angle, and the cold salt spray was tearing at our life jack-ets. The wind was blowing us toward the Atlantic. If we missed Sandy Hook, the next landfall was Ireland.

I was telling Gabe in as calm a voice as I could muster, "Everything's okay. . . . We're under control. . . . This is all perfectly normal . . ." But in my mind, I was scream-ing, "What am I doing here?"

That's an excellent question. What on God's green, dry, blessedly solid earth, was I, a landlubber from Missouri, doing out in the middle of Raritan Bay in a sailboat? The water, which one thinks of as a liquid, slippery, gliding sort of substance, felt like a plowed field with lots of big rocks. The sail, which had begun as a placid triangle, was now straining its stitches with a bellyful of wind. I found that turning the boat around was impossible. The best i could hope for was catastrophe. My normally nimble mind was caught in something like vapor lock. Panic seized my heart, and fear was the controlling element of your every move.

As I sat there in the stern of my new three-thousand–dollar toy, mentally proofreading my obituary, all my mistakes popped into vivid focus for me. When we had arrived that morning, I had seen only the brilliant blue skies, the warm sunshine, the flags snapping merrily in the breeze.

"What a perfect day for a sail" I had exulted to Gabe.

We put the boat in the water, stepped the mast, and rigged all the lines. I had studied well the night before, and I could name every cleat and halyard. Yes, I had noticed that there were no other sailboats out, but a Midwestern transplant to New York is merely glad to be away from the crowd at last. When we cast off from the dock, I took one last look at the flag on top of the yacht club, just to get the direction of the wind. When we left the lee of the building and the wind first struck our sail, I suddenly deduced why, perhaps, that flag was a bright red.

A sailboat is a wonderful teacher of humility. Being driven at thirty knots toward the North Atlantic by a deadly combination of meteorology, physics, and ignorance can have a withering effect on one's self-esteem. To salvage what was left, I had to get us back to the dock alive. I had to turn that boat around. But I could not bring her bow through the powerful wind. I tried several times to bring her about, but to no avail. We were still hurtling downwind like a bathtub lurching down a marble staircase.

Finally, novice sailor that I was, I attempted a jibe—that is, bringing her stern through the wind. Big mistake. The boat capsized, the sail smacking down on the water like a drunk hitting the barroom floor, tossing us into the water. We bobbed to the surface in our yellow life vests. (The only thing we'd done right was to buy those vests). The water was cold, but when I looked over at Gabe, she was laughing for the first time that day. I swam over and asked if she was all right. "I'm fine!" she said, "Not scared any more. The worst has happened, and we're still alive!"

Now we were in the icy water clinging to the bottom of the capsized boat, trying to grow suction cups on our fingers (there is nothing so slippery as the bottom of a fiberglass sailboat). As we bobbed up and down with the big waves—up and down - we felt something odd through the hull—a kind of "boink" as the boat reached the bottom of a trough. Boink. Boink. "What is that?"

At last I figured it out: Our mast was twenty feet long and was now pointing straight down. Apparently, Raritan Bay was only eighteen feet deep at that point, so it was a bad day for some clams, as well, innocent bystanders that they were . . . or should I say innocent bivalves? Soon, the bent mast fell out of its socket and floated up beside the boat, the blue-and-white sail billowing around us like a Dacron jellyfish.

Fortunately, although there were no other sailboats out, there were motorboats. A large cabin cruiser had seen us and chugged up to the rescue: a dentist from Maplewood, New Jersey and his family, out for the first cruise of the year. They took us aboard, gave us dry towels and whiskey. One of the dentist's daughters, a girl of about twelve, asked if we were hungry, and offered us a Trisket cracker topped with cheese from an arosol can.

They towed us back to the yacht club dock. There, a group of the club members, in their Nautica jackets and Docksiders,were shaking their heads and tut-tutting. I thanked our rescuers, and we got the sailboat's hull flipped over and back on the trailer.

The mast looked like a mangled coat hanger. We lost the tiller, the centerboard, and my pants. My wallet would be sent to me the following February, found by a guy walking the beach at Sandy Hook. The wallet looked like it had been swallowed and regurgitated by a squid. It's a miracle that the driver's license and a couple of credit cards were still in it. My pants probably washed up in Ireland.

This ugly event is decades old now, but the feelings are as indelible as the ink on the insurance claim. I tell it to you now to illustrate the ancient idea that calamity is the midwife of comedy. "Sweet are the uses of adversity," Shakespeare wrote, and one of the uses is to find entertaining stories to laugh at in retrospect.

## Vocal Exercise

To paraphrase my good friend and master voice coach Dennis Carlo Patella, tension is the enemy of resonance, sloppiness, the enemy of clear diction. Here are some exercises that will, if practiced regularly, give you a stronger, more nimble tongue.

- Try lapping like a cat; run your tongue in and out of your mouth as rapidly as possible.
- Extend your tongue and try to touch first the tip of your nose, then your chin.
- Repeat the words, ARed leather, yellow leather@ five times as rapidly as you can.

Pronounce the following phrases carefully, paying special attention to the action of the tongue:

- Truly rural
- The rat ran over the roof of the house
- Lovely lilies grew along the lake
- Alone, alone, all, all alone

Consistent attention to your articulation can make a tremendous difference to the clarity of your speaking. Your audiences will appreciate it.

## Something to Ponder

"The aim of a joke is not to degrade the human being but to remind him that he is already degraded."

—George Orwell

## 12 — On Modern Art

*"In every work of genius we recognize*
*our own rejected thoughts;*
*they come back to us*
*with a certain alienated majesty."*
—Ralph Waldo Emerson

When I first came to New York years ago, I was eager to learn more about modern art. As soon as I could afford it, I joined the Museum of Modern Art on 53rd street in Manhattan, and I went there as often as possible. I ran right to the masterpieces, and quickly chose favorites, which I visited often: *Starry Night* by Van Gogh, the sculptures of Brancusi and Nadleman, Monet's *Waterlilies . . .* among many others.

Soon, though, I began to wonder about some of the other paintings I was hurrying past, paintings that made little sense to me. Some of them were downright ugly, I thought. What was the big deal about Picasso? De Kooning must be a spastic; Matisse drew like an 8-year-old; and Jackson Pollack was obviously a self-indulgent egomaniac—I was not surprised to learn that he died in a car wreck while driving drunk. Still, here were all these smart, educated New Yorkers who seemed to appreciate these artists. I also noticed that my favorites were the easy stuff, the ones most often surrounded by the tourists from the Midwest . . . where I came from. It caused me to wonder, "Am I missing something?"

One day I decided to ignore my favorites and look for the pieces I didn't like. Soon I had assembled a list of stuff I thought was lousy. I figured I'd start at the bottom. Which of these paintings did I hate the most? I picked one by Jackson Pollack. Back in the early 1950s, Pollack had developed what he called "action painting." He laid huge canvases on the floor and just dripped and dribbled paint on them, threw the paint around, went wild with it. The things wound up just chaotic scribbles of color. "Okay," I said to myself, "I'm going to figure this guy out."

I stood in front of the largest Pollack and looked. I realized then that I had never actually stood still and looked at it before. I usually found it so repellant that I hurried on by, as you might avoid a puddle of something disgusting on the sidewalk. Now I tried to drop my judgment and just accept it, see what was there. It was big—enough canvas for a good-sized sailboat—with five or six colors of paint: drips and lines, spatters and drools. There was no hint of a brush mark or any other indication that this paint was under anyone's control. I realized that Pollack had actually been very careful not to touch the canvas.

I decided to time myself. Two minutes at a distance of six feet. Soon, the colors began to separate for me. I saw all the white drips, and then all the green and brown, and so on. After 30 seconds I had to step back a few feet as the colors took on patterns which seemed to move and swirl. I grew dizzy. The paint was throbbing on my eyes. Was this vertigo? I began to hyperventilate. I had to sit down. I suddenly felt as though I were looking down at a strange planet from thirty-thousand feet. I could feel the wind rush by and the immense depth and transparency of the air between me and the surface. I no longer saw it as paint on canvas but as some natural phenomenon like the Grand Canyon or the bark of a eucalyptus tree. It was fantastic.

Later, when I described it to a friend, our conversation went like this:

She: It sounds frightening.

I: Yes, I was a bit terrified . . . and in those few minutes, my whole idea of art changed. I'm no longer content just looking for pictures—now I'm looking for feelings, experiences. That painting may make you uncomfortable, but you cannot look at it without feeling something.

She: I don't know if I like that. For me, an art work should be comforting—if not beautiful, at least not threatening—and always visually meaningful.

I: That's fine. Many people—most people feel the same way.

She: I need the element of skill to enjoy an artwork. Pollack, Motherwell, de Kooning don't show me much. They just slap it on. And there are others who just put up a totally black canvas, or a single solid color. That's too easy. What's the point?

I: Perhaps they just want to get us past that question. What's the point of anything, when you come down to it? Perhaps it's enough to just inhabit this instant of time with the feelings we have without the need to attach some meaning to it. To find what the Zen masters refer to as "suchness".

She: I like meaning.

I'll leave this conversation here. It has continued, intermittently, for many years, through many changes of the cast, without arriving at any satisfactory conclusion that all parties could agree on.

## Speaker's Tip

The important item in that story is the question, "Am I missing something?" I find when that question occurs to me, the answer must be, "Yes." Luckily, I jotted this episode and its insights down in my notebook, which is the tip I want to offer now.

We all miss things every day, every moment, and that is why we should all carry notebooks. I suggest you open your notebook when the "Am I missing something?" question comes up, and record the "suchness" of the moment. Then, years later, when you're in your study and feeling in a reflective frame of mind, you can open the notebook again and draw, if not an absolute conclusion, at least a sort of emotional subtotal.

When we step before an audience to speak from our experience, our speeches will be worthier if our experiences have been captured in our notebooks until they've had a chance to ripen and be tasted, seasoned, and tasted again, before they are served.

### Something to Ponder

"We are the caterpillars of angels."
—Vladimir Nabokov

## 13 – Leadership

*"Our chief want in life is having someone who will make us do what we can."*
—Ralph Waldo Emerson

When I was in high school back in Farmington, Missouri, I got a job in the local dry goods and clothing store. The store's owner was a sweet-natured man named Herb who wanted to instill in all his staff the importance of good customer service. One day, a man with only one leg came in to buy a pair of trousers. Herb, seeing an opportunity to demonstrate going the extra mile, took the customer himself while we clerks stood by to observe. Herb measured the man's waist and ran back to the stock room, where he found the required trousers. Then, thinking he would suit the customer by customizing, he took out scissors and cut off one of the trouser legs. When he got back to the customer, he discovered he had cut off the wrong leg.

Leadership is difficult. Ironically, poor Herb probably taught a stronger, more effective lesson by fouling up than he would have by getting it right. Lead by example, the slogan goes, but it doesn't say by *good* example, does it? In a negative way, Herb had reinforced the old carpenter's axiom to measure twice and cut once. It's a cinch that none of us clerks who witnessed that event would ever use scissors on trousers.

Public speaking makes all of us leaders, and that bestows responsibility. There are two chief drivers or motivations for leaders: love and power. These two play an intricate dance with each other in creating the fabric of an organization. If there is a single definition of a leader, it can only be "one whom others follow." It's wonderful how the leader always depends on the followers, isn't it? Even the totalitarian must persuade the population that he belongs at the top of the fear chain.

The power element, at its most basic, is the power that the followers lend to the leader; it is only a loan. Think of Mussolini. For years, he enjoyed the power and love of his countrymen who saluted him as "Il Duce," "Supreme Leader." After Anzio, it was clear to the Italians which way the wind blew; Il Duce's support folded like a lawn chair, and he had to run to the Germans for protection from his own people. He had lost the image of invincibility, so he lost his following.

What would you say are the primary skills required of a leader? The abilities to teach, inspire, motivate, direct, model, create new visions, infect others with enthusiasm and optimism, focus attention, persuade, sell, innovate, clarify, coach, empathize, fail and recover, persevere. . .? The list could go on. But are these actually skills, or are they qualities, character traits? Isn't there a genuine skill behind all these? How is anyone to know a leader possesses these qualities unless it is by a skill for communicating to others? Communication might be called a "meta-skill," the ability upon which all the other talents of leadership must rest.

The strongest communication anyone can make as a leader, follower, speaker, or listener comes from being. Herb continued to be an effective leader even though we employees laughed and shook our heads at the trouser incident, because there was something endearing, vulnerable, and human there. I think of Herb when I remember the 2000 Presidential campaign. George W. Bush was seen as more human and accessible by his followers because of his many failures and fumbles as a speaker, compared to the polished, rehearsed, automaton-like Al Gore.

## Speaker's Tip

Leaders must speak in visual terms. Audiences cannot make a picture of concepts, abstractions, or dry statistics. Audiences need to be able to see what you mean to follow your lead. The best visions are carried by stories. We listen better to stories; they are easier to remember. Remember that Jesus spoke in parables - and not, as some wags have suggested, simply because he lacked statistics.

The most successful politicians, preachers and business leaders will find stories to carry their message. This is why it has become a tradition for Presidents, when delivering the State of the Union Address every year, to invite a few of the "common people" to illustrate a point of policy. When you are writing your speech, be cautious of overusing abstractions, statistics, and generalizations. Words like integrity and freedom may give your message a high tone, but they cannot elicit mental pictures in your audience by themselves.

Good writing, and good speaking, for that matter, must stimulate the imagination by providing images in the minds of readers and listeners through the use of illustrations. My college writing text lists four forms of illustration: developed examples, evidence, anecdotes, and scenarios. Their function is to make your writing, and therefore your speaking, more persuasive, specific, and concrete . . . and more memorable.

### Something to Ponder

"Leadership is the ability to decide what has to be done and then get people to *want* to do it."
—Dwight D. Eisenhower

*"Most folks are about as happy
as they make up their minds to be."*
—Abraham Lincoln

An article in the *NY Times* says that even economists are beginning to study the meaning and quantity of "happiness." In the tradition of the dismal science, economists are trying to determine if money plays a role in people's happiness. They find it does—no surprise there—but not as much as it should. "Money does buy happiness," said an economist at Dartmouth, "It just hasn't bought enough."

"Life, liberty and the pursuit of happiness" . . . . Jefferson had the right idea. Or did he? Happiness chased is an ever-receding horizon. In *Man's Search for Meaning,* Viktor Frankl wrote, "It is a characteristic of American culture that, again and again, one is commanded and ordered to 'be happy.' But happiness cannot be pursued; it must ensue."

Happiness cannot be sought, it must be found indirectly. This reminds me of something my brother, an astronomer, told me once: When looking through a telescope at a very dim object, an experienced astronomer will intentionally look away from the object and observe it with peripheral vision. It takes great training and discipline to look away from the object you seek; but the arrangement of rods and cones on the human retina are capable of a much finer resolution in one's peripheral field of view. In the same way, happiness is on the periphery of our intention in life. If we strive for it directly, we may find a form of happiness, but it will not have the resolution, the quality of that happiness that arises as a by-product.

If we look at the etymology of the word "happy," we find that it derives from the Middle English "hap," which meant chance. This is evident with our word "happen," which has the absence of intention we need when making the excuse "it just happened." The presence of chance in the root of "happy" puts happiness in the realm of luck, which seems fitting, because the economists aren't able to lay claim to it. The question remains: if we find a shortage of happiness in our lives, how are we to get more? Can't buy it. Can't even pursue it. No wonder so few people in this cockamamie world are happy.

At this point in my life, my happiness is gathered in the person of our seven-year-old daughter, Elizabeth. She is a remarkable person. From early in her life, she displayed an optimism, joy, and capacity for caring that gladdens the hearts of those who meet her. When she was only a few months old, sitting on a couch with several other infants, one of whom was bawling in distress, Elizabeth reached over and comforted the crying child with gentle strokes.

Her fondest activity seems to be to making presents for others. She will work for hours to create a treasure hunt for my wife, Peggy, and me to find in the morning. There is no need for a special occasion—it can be any common sort of Tuesday morning as we go around the living room to search out little folded scraps of paper with hearts drawn on them, crayon Xs and Os for "hugs" and "kisses." There will be pictures of gardens and of sunshine, and crudely cut-and-stapled crowns for us to wear as we eat our breakfast. Through these searches, Elizabeth is the very personification of joy, laughing and clapping and jumping around with boundless energy, delighted that she has indeed surprised and pleased us.

I trouble you with these descriptions not simply to brag on my child and my good fortune in having her, though I readily admit the pleasure it gives me to do so but also to underscore the point made by Viktor Frankl and so many others: that happiness ensues. Ah, yes, but ensues from what? My experience is that we feel most gratified when we have given our efforts toward some creative work or play that takes our attention off ourselves. Elizabeth's joy arose from the joy she brought to others.
True happiness, it seems to me, is the result and byproduct of love. Elizabeth is a happy person, not because she has tried to be happy, but because she has simply expressed her natural impulse to love.

A speaker I heard recently told a story about heaven and hell. It seems a man was given a tour of both places. His guiding angel took him to hell, where people sat around a banquet table laden with every sort of delicious food and drink but were unable to enjoy this bounty because their arms were locked in a full extension, and they could not bend them to carry food to their mouths. They sat around the tantalizing feast, helpless, hungry, and frustrated. Then the angel showed his guest heaven. Here again, the banquet table was set with every manner of delicacy, and here again, the people's arms were locked and useless to them. But here they were happy; they had learned to feed one another.

To express your self well is a gift. But like any gift, it must be for the benefit of the receiver. If we share our power and capability with our audiences generously and authentically, we have given them a gift of entertainment, or knowledge, or inspiration. Be happy for those moments when you have the power to give, for every true gift contains love at its core.

## Speaker's Tip

When we think of vocal variety, many of us imagine a speaker performing a dialogue among several people, changing his voice for each character and making a virtuoso performance of it all. In fact, there is a great deal of variety to be found in normal conversation, which, if carried to the lectern, will serve the speaker quite handsomely.

To acquire this knack, one first needs to listen with a fine ear. Do you notice the many changes in tempo of an intelligent conversationalist who is telling a story and telling it well? Can you discern the little pauses, rests, and hesitations between the words, how they lend emphasis and gravity to certain words while tossing others away? This is the mark of a fine speaker, to my mind.

The journeyman speaker will have worked his piece out thoroughly and sort of homogenized it for his audience until it flows at a consistent pace. The expert storyteller will leave the tempo a bit lumpy, with the more dramatic moments being slower; a longer pause after the punch line; a graceful sketchiness to get through the obvious stuff. My advice is to leave pitch alone and concentrate on tempo if you want to lend interesting vocal texture to your next speech.

### Something to Ponder

"Things may come to those who wait, but only the things left by those who hustle."
—Abraham Lincoln

*"Music is your own experience,*
*your thoughts, your wisdom.*
*If you don't live it, it won't come out your horn."*
—Charlie Parker

In the wonderful book, *Flow*, Mihaly Csikszentmihalyi cites a study done by a team of Italian researchers in the Swiss Alps. In this study, the team found a whole village of people who never work. Or maybe they never *stop* working. It's hard to tell. They're in a constant state of flow, a state of happy, contented absorption in whatever task is before them, as in "going with the flow." It isn't work, so it must be play.

Play is the process by which new ideas come into the world. The ascent of the human race began with a bunch of hairy primates sitting around playing with fire. Playing is an essential element in all creativity—in the business world, the modern stress on innovation has brought about a phenomenon I call "productive play." What is productive play? Play that works. Do you play at work? Is work ever fun? Let's consider the value of play and how we can get more of it into our lives and work.

I believe Corporate America needs to pay more attention to the value of play. More and more companies are discovering what Southwest Airlines has found out: Happy, playful workers are more productive, make customers happy, and don't want to leave for other places. No turnover problem there. According to *Fortune* magazine, Southwest Airlines is one of the most sought-after employers in America. In 1999, they got 150,000 applications for fewer than 4,000 jobs. (That's almost as difficult a ratio as the acting business.)

Too many corporations in this country are laboring under the misconception that work should be unpleasant and hard and that if you're having any fun—if you are daydreaming, for instance—you are just goofing off.

Let me put in a plug for daydreaming. Another term for it might be "mind play," because that's what we are really doing when we daydream. We play in our minds. Every invention, every work of art, every original bit of human ingenuity from the needle's eye to night baseball began with mind play. We all know about Sir Isaac Newton and the apple. Well, what do you suppose he was doing sitting under that apple tree in the first place? That's right . . . daydreaming.

Or what about the patent office clerk in Zurich back at the turn of the twentieth century? Every day, he would take his lunch in the square, sit on a bench in the sun, close his eyes, and daydream that he was riding on a beam of that sunlight, holding his pocket watch. His name was Albert Einstein, and his daydream became the theory of relativity.

I read that Corporate America is searching everywhere for the secret of increased productivity, the key to customer service, the end of costly turnover of human resources and that the most valuable assets a company can develop are fresh ideas. Is the answer obvious only to me?

So how do we play at work? Take a tip from the improvisational theater, the daredevils of the acting profession. Improv acting companies like Chicago's Second City, which has fed much talent to TV and the movies, have a simple rule that allows the unfettered playfulness necessary to create their hilarious art. That rule is "yes, and . . ." The actor must accept what is offered. No blocking, no arguments, and no directing the other actors.

I recommend watching *Whose Line Is it, Anyway?* on television, where you'll see this wacky art performed by consummate professionals. It's amazing what the human mind can conceive once the critical authorities are out of the room. Creativity is a function of the right side of the brain—the mute, intuitive, aesthetic, here-and-now self that cohabits every head alongside the critical, nagging voice of the left side, which is usually telling us we should be doing something more practical.

For an excellent course on making the voluntary shift from your left brain to your right brain, I suggest teaching yourself to draw by reading *Drawing on the Right Side of the Brain* by Betty Edwards. This marvelous book, filled with wisdom, inspiration, and insight, is subtitled *A Course in Enhancing Creativity and Artistic Confidence*. If you are a person convinced, as I was, that the ability to draw was genetically denied to you, there is a wonderful surprise waiting for you in these pages. You will learn to see the world as if for the first time and to understand yourself in two new ways.

One of the important concepts Ms. Edwards offers in her book is the notion that the right side of the brain is the part of us that is in touch with the here and now. This is the Buddha mind sought in Zen monasteries, the place where Joseph Campbell said we encounter the eternal.

The left side of the brain, by contrast, is never in the present moment. It exists in only the past or the future—where it can plan, anticipate, dread, regret, analyze, recall, etc. Certainly, we need these skills and feelings, but we also need to learn to live in flow, as those villagers in the Alps do. How do you get into flow? Csikszentmihalyi says you need a compelling goal and you need to be in touch with the present. This is a good blend of both sides of the brain—the left to set a goal, and the right to work in the present moment and accept whatever goal is arrived at.

### Something to Ponder

"Satisfaction of one's curiosity is one of the greatest sources of happiness in life."

—Linus Pauling

# 16 — Persistence

*"I am firm; you are obstinate; he is a pig-headed fool."*
—Bertrand Russell

As the 20th century now rests with the Titanic, we survivors cling to whatever floats and hope for some last insight that will redeem that most ghastly and magnificent of human centuries. What can possibly save us? What have we learned? I think our lesson can be reduced to two words: We persist. All our literature and art, all our religious and philosophical teachings, echo that theme.

To my mind, one work of art that expressed the human condition in the 20th century is Samuel Beckett's great play *Waiting for Godot*. In this bleak, black comedy, a pair of Chaplinesque tramps are waiting along a roadside in the middle of nowhere, for the appearance of someone named Godot, whom they hope will bring them . . . what? Salvation? Redemption? Beckett does not come to our aid any more than Godot comes to the tramps. At the end of the play, Godot sends word that he will not come today, "but surely tomorrow." We find ourselves strangely moved by these sad, heroic clowns. They take turns entertaining themselves and us; they contemplate suicide, they despair, and they recover, laugh. They persist. Elsewhere, Beckett wrote, "Try again. Fail again. Fail better."

The 19th century counterpart to Beckett's masterpiece might be Charles Dickens' *A Christmas Carol*. Dickens brings us Scrooge, a bleak and pitiless man who persists in a world filled with resources; Beckett shows us resourceful characters in a bleak and pitiless world. It's hard to call this progress, but at least we can find some consistency. We have to wonder where this will take us in the next hundred years.

Dickens puts Scrooge through a long night of the soul and wakes him to send a Christmas goose to Bob Cratchett and Tiny Tim. That is Dickens's message of Christmas—Where there's life, there's hope, so persist. All religions have that theme at the root—who is as persistent as Buddha? Or the endlessly dancing Shiva? Go to Egypt, and you will find insistent evidence of an afterlife among animal-headed gods with human hearts who inspired the Pyramids, which persist still through the millennia.

Persistence is in our nature, but that doesn't mean that it's easy. It takes courage. In Spain they test bulls for courage by sending them up against a "picador" on a heavily padded horse. As the bull, in obedience to its nature, charges the horse, the man sticks him in the neck with a spear. The bulls that quit and run from the picador are sent to the slaughterhouse. Those that persist are brought to the arena and given a day of glory on the sand.

We want to step back from this brutal show and say, like civilized Americans, that the bull is in a poor position to appreciate the honor of the thing. But if we examine this a bit closer, we see that the lesson is for us, not the bull. Every Spaniard empathizes with the animal and admires the courage with which it persists in following its nature. Because we are all bound to become dead meat one way or the other, let us take our inspiration from those who have the courage to persist into the very spears of life. There lies our redemption.

When I was fifty-one years old, I became a father for the first time. My little daughter, Elizabeth (Betsy), is the most optimistic, full-of-life and eagerly persistent creature I have ever known. Before she was two, she was providing us with inspiration. In her room, which was next to ours, we had a monitor so we could hear her if she needed us in the night. She proved to be an early riser, often waking with the dawn.

We would hear her stir awake and exclaim in a voice filled with wonder and surprise, "It a new day!" Then she would toddle into our room like a little pink-and-blonde rooster to announce the wonderful news. "It a new day!" For weeks, this continued. Morning after morning, we'd hear her gasp and exclaim, "It happened again!" Then she'd be peeping over the edge of our bed, like a little Eve on her third day in Eden, eyes wide with wonder. "It a new day!"

That's the first generation of the 21st century speaking. We could hardly hope for better than a whole generation of such bright heralds of the dawn. It should inspire us as speakers, too. Let us encourage and promote optimism, provide a little relief to that fraction of humanity that is our audience by helping lighten their spiritual load. Because it takes courage to live, we need encouragement to persist, to persevere, and to insist on living each new day.

My little daughter has grown older, and the sunrise has lost some of its wonder. "It a new day" no longer greets us at dawn, but there are still lessons that jump up out of her mind like little Pop-Tarts of linguistic wisdom. When she was four, helping me in my workshop, she proudly announced to her mommy, "I'm daddy's insistent!" That is a perfect description of her role in my life.

### Something to Ponder

Persistence

Nothing in the world can take the place of Persistence.
Talent will not; nothing is more common than
unsuccessful men with talent.
Genius will not; unrewarded genius is almost a proverb.
Education will not; the world is full of educated
derelicts.
Persistence and determination alone are omnipotent.
—Calvin Coolidge

*"Happiness is good health and a bad memory."*
—Ingrid Bergman

*"One who has perfected the twin arts of remembering and forgetting is in a position to play at battledore and shuttlecock with the whole of existence."*
Soren Kierkegaard

My first memory is of playing a game of catch with my grandmother before I turned two. Grandma was there to take care of me while mother was busy giving birth to my brother. I was standing with Grandma in the front yard of our small house in El Paso, Texas. There was a cotton field across the road, and Grandma and I plucked some of the raw cotton from the stiff, burst-open husks. There were seeds amidst the oily white fibers. With some scraps of material, Grandma sewed a soft, patch-work ball stuffed with our cotton. She held the ball toward me. "Ready?" she asked. "Wedly," I replied and grasped at the soft ball. For the rest of her life, the word "wedly" would be Grandma's code word for her love of me.

Of course this is not a pure memory; it has been aug-mented, revised, and edited by a hundred dinner table repetitions, along with the other family tales. Like the one about my brother's first rubber band or the time Dad and his fraternity brothers shaved a cow; or the story of Grandpa trapped in the flooded mine. These, and many more, have become the Landrum family legends, living, growing, and evolving. No human memory can remain pure, certain, and reliable—we are analog, not digital. Just look at the mistaken "eyewitness accounts" that put people in the slammer—thank God for DNA testing.

We all cherish memory as a way to recover our youthful wonder. Picasso tried for years to paint like a child. . . . Perhaps that's why he so often acted like one. The blessing of memory is that we can attempt to relive those lost moments with the enhancement of our current wisdom and sophistication. The curse of memory is that we cannot relive those lost moments *without* the colorizing influence of our current knowledge and cynicism.

In a way, we create our lives as a writer creates a book, out of memory and imagination. The important thing is to get the proportions right. Memory is safe and comfortable, but it tends to stifle us. Imagination pulls us into the future with its myriad possibilities, which are often risky and sometimes frighten us. The guiding tool is impulse. The track our lives takes depends on which of them, memory or imagination, is allowed to steer our impulses.

Lately, my mother and I have been playing with a set of her memories and creating something new with them. When she was 20 years old, she and her sister Blossom left their home in Joplin, Missouri, and went to spend a year in Italy with their other sister, Harriet. The year was 1938. My mother kept a diary that noted the events of that year. She and I together have recast her memoir in a book titled *Americanata*.

Memories are always and only created in the present. Mom and I created her memoir together—she providing the events and experiences, and I providing the language. It was a strange transplantation of one person's memory into another person's head, which was then retranslated into a third, hybrid memory for the reader. Here is the way one of Mom's early memories of her childhood in northern Wisconsin came out:

"A night that stands out in my mind was in the winter I was five. After the evening meal, my father had to walk to a distant neighbor's house to get some potatoes, and he asked Blossom and me to go with him. Mother bundled us into leggings, galoshes, heavy coats, stocking caps, and mittens. She wrapped wool scarves around our necks and over our faces, leaving only our eyes exposed. Thus prepared for the cold night air, we sat on our sled, a beautiful new Red Ryder, and Daddy began to pull us over the smooth, snow-covered streets to get the potatoes.

"The evening was moonless; the air was cold, still, and sparkling clear. There were no streetlights in our little town, and stars in the millions glittered close overhead against the velvety black sky. It was probably my earliest extended look at them, and I gazed up in wonder. Our breath came like steam through our scarves.

The only sound was the crunch and squeak of Father's footsteps and the hissing runners of our sled in the snow.

"Blossom and I waited the few minutes it took Daddy to get the potatoes, pay for them, and bring the big burlap bag back to the sled. The night was bitter cold, so to keep the potatoes from freezing, he had the two of us sit on the bag to keep it warm. We had a lap robe around our legs that we tucked under the potatoes, keeping them as toasty and snug as we were.

"Some moments of childhood have an indelible power. Their vivid poignancy can be recalled to give us pleasure again and again. That winter evening is just such a memory for me. Blossom on the sled behind me, her arms around my waist; Daddy's strong back, pulling us over the crackling snow; the lumpy potatoes beneath me, and the distinct stars overhead—this memory gives me still a feeling of safety and joy."

## Great Speeches Remembered

"Much has been given to us, and much will rightfully be expected from us. We have duties to others and duties to ourselves; and we can shirk neither. We have become a great nation, forced by the fact of its greatness into relations with other nations of the earth, and we must behave as beseems a people with such responsibilities. Toward all other nations, large and small, our attitude must be one of cordial and sincere friendship. We must show not only in our words, but in our deeds, that we are earnestly desirous of securing their good will by acting toward them in a spirit of just and generous recognition of all their rights. . . . No weak nation that acts manfully and justly should ever have cause to fear us, and no strong power should ever be able to single us out as a subject for insolent aggression."

—Theodore Roosevelt

# 18 — Mom

*"No pessimist ever discovered the secrets of the stars,
or sailed to an unchartered land,
or opened a new doorway for the human spirit."*

—Helen Keller

Back in 1967 when I was in the Army, I phoned my parents to tell them that I had orders for Vietnam. My mother's reaction was, "Well, isn't it nice that you'll be able to see that part of the world." This was a typical example of positive thinking from her. I used to tell that story on her in derisive tones to show how out of touch with reality she was. We often referred to her as our Pollyanna. Now that I'm a parent myself, at last, I've changed my mind. I can see how desperately she wanted to re-frame the reality of war into a harmless adventure for me. And because I came home safe and whole, who knows? Maybe she did.

I hope I grow old like my mom, Becky Landrum. She's 84 now and the busiest person I know. I just got off the phone with her, and I feel like I have to catch my breath. Yesterday morning she hosted her radio talk-show with her dear friend, Ann. The show's called *Our Two Cents*. They do it every Monday morning at the local station in Farmington, Missouri, which is a small town 65 miles south of St. Louis. Mom's lived there for the past 40 years, and she seems to know everybody in the county.

The mayor called her up a while back and asked if she would attend a meeting on the subject of starting a farmer's market. She said sure and came to the courthouse expecting to find a whole committee of people. There was the mayor, one farmer, and her, so she became the manager of the new farmer's market. On Saturdays, she gets up at 6 a.m. and rings the bell to open the farmer's market in the parking lot of the VFW hall. They're in their third year now, and business is booming. Mom now has 27 farmers and several tons of fresh produce every week.

Then there's her work at the hospital. My dad was one of the prime movers in building the hospital, and Mom helped organize the candy-stripers, volunteer women who work on the place the way a top grade motor oil works on a car engine. In addition to their other vital work with patients, doctors, and staff, they started a gift shop. Mom still makes flower arrangements every week to sell there, the proceeds going to worthy projects.

She's been a life-long Sunday painter, and now she's taking a new portrait class with a great art teacher out at Mineral Area College—another institution my dad was instrumental in getting off the ground. Her favorite subjects are her grandchildren—we just got another oil painting of our daughter, Elizabeth, age seven. It's a sunny canvas, filled with love and daffodils. And now there's a new subject on the family tree—great-granddaughter Grace, born last month to my nephew, Michael, and his lovely wife, Andrea. I expect Mom's started sketching from the photos already.

Mom's favorite place to be is still on the golf course. Last year, she cleaned up in the Ladies-Day tournaments— walked off with a couple hundred dollars' worth of prizes for shooting "the best in the worst class." For 50 years now, she has been a deep-dyed student of the great game. She used to keep a five-iron in the kitchen so she could practice her swing while the pot roast simmered. Once, she took a divot out of the linoleum in front of the sink. There are also a few golf clubs in her bedroom just in case a sudden insight about her grip or her backswing should come to her in a dream. Poor Dad woke up in the middle of the night once and found her standing at the foot of the bed brandishing a two-wood over her head. He almost had a coronary.

Dad actually did pass on in 1997, after 57 years of marriage and five hard, suffering years of illness. Mom dealt with the grief in her typical fashion—she got busy. She spent some time with her siblings. She was the youngest of four children, and they were all still around, so she visited them. Her oldest sister, Harriet, was 89 and in poor health in Italy, so Mom went over for a visit.

This brought back memories of 1938, when she and her third sister, Blossom, had lived in Milan with Harriet's family. Mom still had the diary and scrapbooks from that amazing year, and she began to write about it. Her grandchild, Brianna, responded enthusiastically on hearing about this romantic and exciting episode, and that spurred Mom to greater efforts. She sent me some pages and asked if I thought they were worth working on. I offered to help her with the writing, and away we went.

Now, three years later, we are putting the finishing touches on *Americanata: Three Sisters in Italy—1938*. It runs over 200 pages, including photos, and it's a pretty good read, I think. As a twenty-year-old from Joplin, Missouri, my mom took her first look at the cities of Chicago; Washington, DC; and New York before casting off on a trans-Atlantic liner to North Africa and the Mediterranean. It's fun to look at that time through her fresh eyes.

She met fascinating people, saw Mussolini, learned a lot about art, life, history, and the Italians. She even fell in love with a handsome and wealthy Englishman. World War II was bearing down on Europe, and she witnessed the early tremors and met people desperately seeking shelter from the approaching storm.

Working on the book was a blast. It completely reframed our relationship, and I think we both learned a lot about each other and ourselves. It was an interesting experience to get to know my mother as a courageous, venturesome, vital, young woman, although I realize, on reflection, that her character has traced a consistent, exuberant arc across the years. My message for you today is: Take another look at your parents. Talk to them if you can, and make an effort to know them as they were before you came along. It's a generation-bridging experience.

## Something to Ponder

"It is of practical value to learn to like yourself. Since you must spend so much time with yourself you might as well get some satisfaction out of the relationship."
—Norman Vincent Peale

## Speaker's Tip

Speed-speaking is a nervous reaction that rises from the same logic that says pulling off a band-aid quickly will hurt less. Speed speakers are not considering their hearers, and the audience soon joins them in wishing their speech a quick finish. The cure for speed-speaking is to work on better eye contact and on relishing the words you are speaking. Savor each syllable by imagining a color, taste, and texture for it; give each word its own space and time. Listen to recordings of the spoken word—poetry, plays, stories—read by fine actors like John Guilgud, Judy Dench, Richard Burton. Tune in "Selected Shorts" on National Public Radio on the weekends. The tongue must learn from the ear.

Here's a short passage from Charles Dickens that is excellent for practicing savoring each word:

"Oh, but he was a tight-fisted hand at the grindstone, Scrooge! A squeezing, wrenching, grasping, scraping, clutching, covetous old sinner! Hard and sharp as flint, from whom no steel had ever struck out generous fire; secret and self contained and solitary as an oyster."

## 19 — Being Right

*Being right is of minimal importance—*
*a stopped clock will show the correct time twice a day.*

Anonymous

Some years ago, when I was struggling with the issues that were holding me back—like the need to be right and the need for others' approval—I had an insight. In a day-dream, a sort of trance, I found myself floating in the middle of the Pacific Ocean, as far from land as it is possible to be. It was also the deepest part of the ocean—you could drop Mt. Everest in right there and it would sink without a trace. But I was okay, because I had a buoy, a float that I was clinging to—and I mean clinging for dear life.

Suddenly, a thought occurred to me: What if this buoy I'm clinging to is not a float at all? Suppose it's a weight? What if, rather than holding me up, I'm holding it up? What if it's actually holding me down? Then, if I let go, rather than sink and drown and die, I would rise and soar and fly!

I would like to tell you that this insight cured me of all neurotic need, and I have been lighter than air ever since, but of course you know that isn't true. I struggle to let go of that damn buoy every day. Our perceptions work against us. We believe that the weight is a float, because it was once; and when a belief takes root, it is harder to pull out than an old forsythia bush.

To let go of the need to be right is a difficult thing to do. Admitting you made a mistake seems to become more difficult as a person ascends the ladder of authority; look at the behavior of our presidents. At the other end of the social scale (in a manner of speaking) are the artists for whom mistakes are the tools and instruments of life. All art proceeds by trial and error, and the error is essential. There is a film of Picasso that shows him in the process of creating a large, complex painting. We watch the canvas as the artist paints over the course of a full day, compressed into five minutes or so of screen time. The composition unfolds and evolves; every element, every inch of the canvas gets painted, painted over and repainted in a dizzying parade of images. Masterpieces emerge in one place or another, and we in the audience groan to see them wiped out and replaced. At last, the artist's voice can be heard saying, "I've made a botch of this," and he discards the whole thing and starts over with a fresh canvas. Now, his theme worked out in his mind, he works with great economy and confidence, creating a powerful, unified, and gratifying work of art.

To be willing to let go of "rightness" is to honor process above predetermined result. That may be the greatest lesson we can learn from the arts. "The formula 'Two and two make five' is not without its attractions," wrote Dostoevsky, who made a career of letting go, questioning authority, and challenging assumptions.

Perhaps the thing we cling to most ardently is our judgment. This is the container that houses our rightness and righteousness, and, failing to find perfection, it is the container from which we pour out guilt and critical punishment. This is why Picasso yearned to paint like a child. Children lack that constricting judgment, that superego voice behind the left ear that condemns the performance even as the brush-stroke is being laid on.

Thinking of Picasso, I am reminded of the great retrospective of his work at the Museum of Modern Art 20 years ago. I invited a neighbor's son, Lucas, a well read, sensitive, artistic sort of thirteen-year-old to go along and see it with me. As we walked through the galleries, his reaction to nearly every painting was, "I don't like that one," rendered quickly, with barely a glance at the work in question. I saw then that Lucas was no longer a child. He had discovered the power of judgment and had fortified himself against these challenging, "not right" paintings.

Of course, he was also challenging my judgment, and I felt myself getting defensive. I decided to discuss judgment itself. We took a break and sat in the sculpture garden. "Lucas," I asked, "which of these trees is the best, do you think?"

"I don't know," he replied. "What do you mean, 'the best'?"

"Good question. Would it occur to you to choose one as 'the best' if I hadn't asked you to?"

"I suppose not."

"Probably not. There are wide stretches of life when we don't need our judgment, aren't there?"

"I guess so. Why go around judging clouds and flowers?" he continued. "Who cares?"

"Who cares, indeed," I said. "When we look at nature, we don't judge. We can just accept it and see what's there, can't we?"

"I suppose. . ."

"What would happen if we made a little effort to look at the art with that same point of view?"

I wish I could report success here, but there ensued a long discussion on the necessity of judgment: The artist himself using it, the curators at the museum, the critics, the people who paid such obscene amounts of money for these paintings. I tried to counter with the difference between snap and considered judgment; the blindness and tunnel-vision it enforces; the essentially negative point of view that lies behind judgment. After all, if we like something, we accept it, and acceptance is not the same as judgment.

But there is no prying the hands of a thirteen-year-old from the buoy. I finally let go myself, accepted Lucas's right to his own point of view, and floated happily along an inch or two above the floor, savoring Picasso for the rest of the afternoon. I consoled myself with the thought that being right was only an opinion and that an opinion was a meager accomplishment.

## Something to Ponder

"We receive three educations: one from our parents, one from our schoolmasters, and one from the world. The third contradicts all that the first two teach us."
—Charles, Baron de Montesquieu:

*"The Scots and the Irish leave you close to tears.*
*There even are places where English completely*
*disappears. In America they haven't used it for years."*
—Alan Jay Lerner

We all know the story of *Pygmalion*, the play by G.B. Shaw, that became the hit musical *My Fair Lady* in the talented hands of Lerner and Lowe. Eliza Doolittle, drab street person and seller of flowers, is passed off as royalty at a state ball after being trained to speak properly by one Professor Higgins, misogynist and bachelor. It is great entertainment, and it makes the clearest case in literature for the importance of voice and diction training.

The surest, simplest way to reinvent yourself is with vocal training. Most of us have little or no formal education in proper diction. The voice is taken for granted by almost everyone except singers, radio personalities, and, sometimes (too seldom these days), actors. For the rest of the population, the idea of working on the speaking mechanism never occurs. Only if we hear ourselves recorded do we realize the disparity between our diction and our vocal self-image, and the sometimes harsh truth.

Almost no one speaks with their "natural" voice. A newborn child's voice is a force of nature. An infant can produce a cry at the fullest possible volume and keep it up for hours without becoming hoarse. An adult will often experience discomfort and vocal fatigue by the half-time of an exciting sports event. The infant is screaming for higher stakes than the sports fan. For the baby, it's a matter of life and death that its voice be heard by its mother; its voice comes out clear, pure, and unimpeded. As children, we continue to use our voices well and naturally until we run into the muffling inhibitors set up by parents, teachers, and other grown-ups who take exception to our boundless vocal energy—or noise. That's when all of our natural, childlike urges to sing and shout become stifled.

When you think about it, the human voice is a completely acquired thing. All the tools of speech have other, more important tasks. The lungs, the engine of the voice, are meant primarily to provide oxygen to our blood; the larynx, or "voice-box" as we call it, is actually a valve to prevent food from falling into the trachea; the mouth has several other functions that could take precedence over speech, such as tasting, chewing, drinking, inhaling, and kissing. Look at the development of speech and language, and you see an evolutionary miracle spanning two or three million years. The infant will retrace the entire process in less than two years.

I loved listening to my daughter, Elizabeth, during those first two years. Her first year was filled with every sound the human vocal mechanism is capable of making—the French "R", the German "CH", even the click sounds of central Africa. At about the age of three, she was speaking quite fluently with one or two small, charming idiosyncracies. At least I found them charming. It's a parent thing. Those of you who gag at cuteness should skip the next paragraph.

Elizabeth had difficulty distinguishing certain consonants: hard Gs became Ds, and hard Cs became Ts, so "good cookie" became "dood tookie." Elizabeth could hear the difference, but her articulation let her down. When we would imitate her, she would protest, "No, not dood. Dood!" Eventually, of course, she outgrew this baby talk, and now it takes some effort to be that cute.

Many of us grew to adulthood with a misshapen standard of pronunciation, established by the dialects of our environments. Folks where I come from, southeast Missouri, tend to add an unnecessary vowel sound now and then, but they make up for it by subtracting just about as many vowels and lots of final consonants, too. For instance, they might pronounce "every girl is going" as "ever' gir-ul is goin'." My wife, who comes from central New Jersey, might compress the city of Newark into a single syllable: "Nerk."

Most people glide blithely through life, unconcerned about such apparently trivial matters as regional accent and proper pronunciation. After all, people understand what they say. It's not like they're speaking pig-Latin all the time. And yet, we do judge each other by our accents, don't we?

I recently attended a training of managers in the north-eastern U.S. They watched a video of Zig Ziglar, one of America's foremost business speakers, who comes from Yazoo City, Mississippi. When asked their evaluation of what Ziglar had to say, almost everyone in the room responded that they had difficulty taking him seriously because "he talked like such a hick." Clearly, Ziglar's down-home, grits-'n'-gravy style did not charm these city people. By the same token, the films of Woody Allen do not find a wide appreciation in rural America. I happened to see one some years ago in a 500-seat the-atre in Minnesota. Besides myself, there were three oth-ers in the audience.

So what's the ideal? Well, if you want to appeal to the widest possible audience, you would do well to listen carefully to the news anchors on network TV. These ladies and gentlemen have worked on their diction, knowing that they are speaking to the broadest possible range of people in this country and abroad. Any region-alism in their delivery must be subtle—there's a touch of Texas drawl in Dan Rather's commentary, and if you lis-ten for it, you can still hear a bit of Louisville, Kentucky, when Dianne Sawyer speaks—but few people in any region of this country find these two professionals lack-ing in credibility.

In most things, we are pretty much stuck with the cards that God and our gene pool have dealt us. You can change your looks to some extent with make-up, clothes, fitness regimens, etc., or you can go for painful and expensive surgery that can even alter your gender, but nothing matches the transformation you can make by simply learning to speak clearly, gracefully, and naturally. Just ask Eliza Doolittle.

## Something to Ponder

"If you can talk brilliantly about a problem, it can create the consoling illusion that it has been mastered."

—Stanley Kubrick

*"The world is a vast temple dedicated to discord."*
—Voltaire

*Note: this essay was written in the weeks following September 11, 2001.*

I've known death. It has taken my loved ones—close relatives, dear friends, colleagues, comrades. I once flew home from Saigon in the belly of a mammoth cargo plane with 140 other soldiers. I had the only passenger seat on that flight, facing rearward, next to the ladder to the cockpit. My traveling companions were stacked before me in their aluminum caskets, three deep, five across, stretching back into the depths of that strange, flying cavern. You think you know death after such an experience, but you forget, somehow, so that when it turns up again you're stunned anew by the utter, implacable finality of it. Someone was there and is no more.

We New Yorkers have the additional pain of having lost the most prominent feature of our city. It has been a massive amputation. There is a kind of phantom-limb ache for us when we turn our eyes toward that space where those towers stood. Even those who, like myself, considered them rather banal as architecture now miss them fondly and re-erect them in our mind's eye glistening in the sun, the pair of them soaring more than a quarter of a mile into the skyline. Their absence must be heartbreaking for those who lost loved ones there. Many citizens have expressed the desire to see them rebuilt, as a monument, if nothing else.

It is a disturbing thing to be hated. It causes us to hate in return—a perfectly normal reaction to such insane barbarity. I am glad to hear the word "patience" coming from the President and the administration. I am not glad to hear the word "war." I think it's a big mistake to define our relationship with these lunatics as a war. It gives them far too much honor and status. It lifts them from the criminally insane category and turns them into soldiers and patriots. They are a pack of bigots and outcasts from their own people, forced to live in caves in a remote and reviled country or to sneak furtively through the free world, traitors to the human race.

Shouldn't we think ahead to the outcome we desire? Is what we want only to punish, to feel the sweet, fleeting, narcotic high that comes from exacting revenge? This is short-sighted. Hadn't we better give some thought to our other vulnerabilities? The price we pay for living in a free and open society is to offer an easy target for psychotics and sociopaths.

We need to look at the situation more objectively. We are the ones with the most to lose. We have freedom, territory, comfort, wealth, and a high regard for human life. Our enemy has none of these things. He is a slave to his hatred, landless, living in meager circumstances on borrowed territory, and sees his own life and that of his fellows as a weapon. These enemies are only a few now, and if we can win the moderate Arab states to our side, they will likely remain few. But if we go off half-cocked and start invading places – Syria, Iraq, Iran, Afghanistan have been mentioned – the outcome will be to strengthen their support and their numbers. This is a cunning game of global chess we find ourselves in—and we need to think way ahead. This attack was quite deliberately meant to provoke exactly the reaction we are providing. There is a trap set here, and we need caution, diplomacy, and patience to avoid it.

I

## Something to Ponder

"When myth meets myth, the collision is very real."

—Stanislaw Lec, *Unkempt Thoughts*

*"Directing George C. Scott is a wonderful experience. He follows direction so easily, knowing that wherever he sits, it will be the head of the table."*

—Jose Quintero

We create our selves and our lives. As countless wise thinkers have said, "We are what we think." It's essential to understand that thought is creatable. Many times in my life, I have felt like the helpless victim to my own thoughts, especially the negative, depressing, pessimistic ones.

I once went through a long period of low self-esteem and depression until one day I had the insight that brought me out of it. It began with a saying I first heard in Mexico: "Every head's a world." I saw my own head as a literal globe, a world with oceans, continents, atmosphere, and a molten core of energetic life-force. It was suddenly obvious to me that I had been choosing to live in those parts of my world-head that were gloomy, barren, and depressing. I looked around my head for another place to live and settled on a sunny, friendly island in a warm tropic sea. I decided to create a new life for myself.

"Causa Sui" means "invent yourself," to be at once the cause and the effect. To me, it summons the image of a snake with its tail in its mouth, or M.C. Escher's drawing of hands drawing each other with pencils. It has become my motto (I've decided just now) because I love the image of endlessly beginning again. Our country is at such a place, it seems. Our old assumptions have been blasted to rubble, and we must re-create our selves in new ways and for new purposes.

As I write, it is Halloween, 2001, seven weeks after the attack on the World Trade Towers and the Pentagon. Dressing up for a costume party last night put me in touch with an idea that actors often confront and that "civilians" seldom seem to notice: the importance of exploring your alternate identities. In past centuries, and in some countries still, people celebrate holidays by taking a holiday from their normal personalities. We honor this concept at Halloween by donning masks, taking other personas, and acting in ways completely different from our normal, conventional behaviors. It strikes me that there is a value in this ritual that is not fully appreciated.

Perhaps we Americans place too great an emphasis on "authenticity." We neglect the lessons to be learned from expressing our alternate identities. The danger of going too far in this single identity syndrome is being played out now by these terrorists who plague us with their rigid, narrow, fundamentalist ideas of life, religion, and culture. Walt Whitman spoke for us all (which is the poet's chief function) when he said, "I am large, I contain multitudes." So, indeed, do we all contain a vast array of identities; we shift effortlessly in and out of them like quick-change artists. Most of the time, this shape-shifting passes unnoticed by ourselves and others, but if you stop to think about it, isn't it true that you are one person with your spouse, another with your child, still another with your mother, your boss, the state trooper who pulls you over, your old sweetheart, the IRS auditor, a surly waiter, a pan-handler on the subway . . . and on and on?

This must be true even for those who pride themselves on taking an egalitarian stance toward the world and boast that they "speak to everyone in the same tone of voice." Actors understand that the human personality arises from a process of relationship—who we are depends to some extent on who we're with. It's like the old Norman Rockwell painting that shows several vignettes: first, a man being chewed out by his boss on some office matter, then the man berating his wife for some foul-up at home, then the wife scolding her son for a bad report card, the boy getting mad at his little sister, and finally, the little girl ragging the kitten. Each of us needs to dominate someone, sometime, and we all belong in a huge network of pecking orders.

What use is knowing that? I was making a presentation recently about creating a strong relationship with the audience when the subject of charisma came up. I rashly suggested that charisma was a skill that could be learned. It is a tool that the best speakers, actors, performers, and politicians use to great advantage. We need an example, so I'll summon my favorite lesson-carrier, Sir Laurence Olivier.

A reporter once had an appointment to meet the great

actor in the lobby of the Mayfair Hotel in London. Arriving on time, he looked in every corner of the lobby for Sir Laurence but came up empty. "Ah, well," he thought to himself, "actors are seldom punctual," and he sat down to wait. Fifteen minutes passed. Thirty. Forty-five. After an hour, the reporter decided he had been stood up, and he began to leave. On his way to the door, he glanced again at an elderly gentleman reading the newspaper in the corner, who had been there the whole time. He had such a timid demeanor, almost a submerged personality, that the reporter had dismissed him completely, but yes, on closer inspection, he realized the man was indeed the knight and crown jewel of the English stage. Anyone who has ever seen Olivier on stage has remarked on his magnetism, his vibrant, energetic personality, his charisma. But, as this reporter discovered, charisma was a quality that could be turned off, and Olivier, actually a painfully shy, self-conscious introvert in daily life, chose to keep his charismatic fires banked when moving through the workaday world.

Well, if charisma is something that can be taken off, like a Derby hat, then it can be sought and achieved. How? For actors, it always comes down to making choices. An actor in a play works with two elements: the character as set on the page by the playwright, and the living self of the actor with all its foibles and vulnerabilities. The power an actor brings to the role stems directly from his or her ability to own and reveal the full range of that self, which contains all the potential traits that any human being is heir to.

Robert Cohen, in his book *Acting Power*, writes, "Acting

. . . is the moment-to-moment conquest of death. It is 'playing against' the biggest and profoundest of obstacles . . . which can tie the actor to his deepest source of power. Acting, therefore, is an affirmation of living. It is a positive act. Everything we do in life is an act intended to extend and improve our lives; it is this aspect of behavior, the positive aspect, with which audiences will identify. It is this aspect they will understand."

Jack Nicholson, the superb film actor, says, "I'm at least 75 percent of every character I play. For the rest, I try to find a character's positive philosophy about himself." This positiveness is the key to Nicholson's brilliant "good bad boy" performances, and what character is not a "good bad" character when all is said and done?"

When the actor chooses whole-heartedly to put that good-bad self, warts and all, into the character's situation, to strive with commitment to fulfill the character's tasks, to want what the character wants, then those choices make the performance compelling and powerful for the audience. This power is similar to a laser beam of light, that now ubiquitous staple of light-shows and bar-code readers at the checkout counter. Like a laser, a performance can be concentrated, focused, coherent. Like a laser, a charismatic performance has focus, direction, purpose, and tremendous energy.

Charisma then, or personal magnetism, or stage presence, is a result of coherence and congruency. It comes to those who are undivided against themselves, who "walk their talk." We coaches often talk about "attraction"—there are some people who have cleared up their lives to the extent that what they want and need just seems to come to them effortlessly; they seem to attract success.

We need to explore and acknowledge all the aspects of ourselves—even, or perhaps especially, those traits that we don't like in ourselves. Having integrity does not mean stripping away all the unpleasant character flaws that make us ashamed, but owning them all, folding them into the rich mixture of our personalities. Those flaws and vulnerabilities give the human character its texture and distinguish those who live whole lives in the whole world from the fundamentalists who must make do with only the idea of a self in a reduced and meager world.

### Something to Ponder

"Most actors' problems deal with tension. In a very professional actor the tension is because they haven't made a choice that has taken enough of their mental interest. In other words, they haven't made a vital enough choice; it's not up to a level that will engage their imagination and get them into pretending unselfconsciously."

—Jack Nicholson

*"To be shaken out of the ruts of ordinary perception, to be shown for a few timeless hours the outer and the inner world, not as they appear to an animal obsessed with survival or to a human being obsessed with words and notions, but as they are apprehended, directly and unconditionally, by Mind at Large— this is an experience of inestimable value to everyone and especially to the intellectual."*
—Aldous Huxley, *The Doors of Perception*

I sometimes wish I could give a speech without any words. It's a difficult admission for a writer, speaker, and appreciator of fine language, but words are too much with us, I think. They have become so enmeshed in the fabric of existence that it feels as though they *are* existence. We build our world with words the way my little daughter builds her play world out of toys, convincing herself that these dollies are genuinely her babies. Words are woefully inadequate to make a world; they are much farther from concrete reality than Elizabeth's dolly is from an actual baby, and yet we talk our way through life as if it were the only way to live. Mind chatter. We fill every gap, every tiny instant, with chatter—uttered or not.

Have you ever known someone who just could not shut up? There's a word (of course) for that: logorrhea. It's a sad and irritating condition whereby a person seems to be allergic to silence. Every instant must be commented on, or at least filled with some sort of verbal packing—like excelsior—to insulate everyone in earshot from the actual experience of living that moment. Many people suffer under the illusion that only those moments that are described, judged, and turned into verbal narrative are really experienced. In fact, the opposite is true.

Words are abstractions of the world. They are the symbols and surrogates we have created to pass the world around from one head to another. While it may seem to us that they describe the here-and-now in an instantaneous way, they are always at some remove from the suchness of the world. The play-by-play is not the baseball game.

There is a saying, "You are not the voice in your head; you are the hearer of the voice." I think that "voice" part of our mind, the left hemisphere, the super-ego, is trying to get control, and it just can't seem to manage it. Why? The words set us apart from our existential present moment just a bit, a tiny fraction of a nanosecond, while we write a quick critique of the movie we are living. Isn't that so? Isn't the substance of these word-filled thoughts often a bunch of judgments and frets and worries and regrets, casting back and forth between the past and the future, distant and near? Mind-chatter is a sort of monologorrhea in our brain's left hemisphere where that critical, parental-sounding voice in our head just won't shut up.

That nagging inner critical voice can be deadly for speakers and performers of any stripe. I remember working in an acting class led by Frank Corsaro, the great director, writer, and teacher. After I had finished acting a scene, he told me, "We can see you battling with your inner critic. You are so eager to be good, you cannot permit yourself to simply be, without judging it good or bad at the same time. Acting is the ultimate act of trust in yourself. Good, bad, or otherwise, in this play, this scene, you are the character, and therefore, everything you say and do is perfectly appropriate. Furthermore, if somehow, you were able to succeed in being the perfect performer that your inner critic is demanding, the performance would be dull and dead. What makes any performance compelling is its humanness. The flaws and vulnerabilities that your inner critic finds objectionable are, in fact, the interesting and exciting aspects of any performance."

This wise counsel applies equally well to speakers and anyone else who must perform for others. The moment of the performance requires a commitment to self-trust. Bad acting is almost always bad because it is self-conscious. We can see these poor performers divided from their performance, watching, judging themselves harshly, and it undermines our belief in them. Is that not also true for speakers?

To neutralize the critical voice, we need to learn how to empower the hearer of the voice, don't we? The neglected right hemisphere of our human brain is mute—completely nonverbal. The question becomes, Can you live in that mute, silent half of yourself? I submit that you can, and do—and that it is a great benefit to do so as often as possible. How? By taking up some project—gardening, carpentry, cooking, making music, any sort of work with the hands—and becoming so absorbed in it that you lose all track of time. When you come to the end of such a task and are startled to find that hours have elapsed, then you know you have been living in the timeless moment, on the right side of the brain.

If you examine that experience, you may realize that there was little or no mental chatter happening then. You were in a state of flow, as Mihaly Csikszentmihalyi, author and psychologist, has described in his important books on the subject. This special state, flow, is only accessible from the right hemisphere of the brain, from that part of the human mind that is always and only alive to the present moment. The "hearer," the genuine you, your actual self, resides there. The more value and attention you give to that part of yourself, the more available it will be for the crucial performances of your life, like speeches. For some exercises on developing that part of your mind, I again recommend studying the book *Drawing on the Right Side of the Brain*, by Betty Edwards. You will discover astonishing abilities in yourself, see the world with new eyes, and, as a bonus, learn to draw.

I do not mean for you to throw away the left side of the brain, which has many vital skills and abilities. The ideal is to combine the talents of both the right and left so that harmonious integrated activity ensues. Peak performances always display this undivided concentration of skills from every aspect of the self. We need our entire mind, balanced and equalized like the magnificent stereo system it is. Then we can bring forth the music from the whole orchestra of our creative potential.

## Something to Ponder

"It is in order to really see, to see in ever deeper, ever more intensly, hence to be fully aware and alive, that I draw what the Chinese call "The Ten Thousand Things" around me. Drawing is the discipline by which I constantly rediscover the world. I have learned that what I have not drawn, I have never really seen, and that when I start drawing an ordinary thing, I realize how extraordinary it is, sheer miracle."
—Frederick Franck, *The Zen of Seeing*

## Tips for Speakers

Given that words cannot communicate all, here is a passage from Julius Fast's book *Body Language*, which has some lessons for those of us who communicate with gesture and expression:

> "Dr. Norman Kagan of Michigan State University conducted a study among deaf people. "It became apparent to us that many parts of the body, perhaps every part to some extent, reflect a

person's feeling-state." As an example, talking while moving the hands or playing with a finger ring and moving restlessly were all interpreted by the deaf as nervousness, embarrassment and anxiety. When the eyes and face suddenly "came down," when the person seemed to "swallow back" his expression, or when his features "collapsed" it was interpreted as guilt. Excessively jerky movements were labeled frustration, and a shrinking body movement, as if hiding oneself spelled out depression. Forcefulness was seen as the snapping forward of the head and whole body including the arms and shoulders, and boredom was inferred when the head was tilted or rested at an angle and the fingers doodled. Reflectiveness was linked to intensity of gaze, a wrinkled forehead and a down-cast look. Not wanting to see or be seen was signaled by taking off eyeglasses or looking away.

"The interpretations were accurate . . . body language alone, it seems, can serve as a means of communication if we have the ability to understand it, if we are extremely sensitive to all the different movements and signals."

Are we not sensitive enough? Perhaps not as sensitive as the deaf, but I find few surprises in the descriptions of these gestures. Our feeling state will be transmitted, verbally or not, and most audiences will receive and understand most of the transmissions.

Published in the January 2006 issue of *The Speechwriter's Newsletter* and as a special supplement to *The Executive Speaker*

Speechwriter Dana Rubin, founder and force behind the New York Speechwriters' Roundtable, scored a coup last September by persuading Theodore C. Sorensen to be our lunchtime speaker. For 11 years, Sorensen was a policy advisor, legal counsel, and speechwriter for Senator and then-President John F. Kennedy. The Kennedy administration brought many changes to Washington, D.C. In January 1961, JFK was 43 years old and the first president born in the 20th century.

He surrounded himself with the "best and brightest" young aides and associates the country had to offer, chief among them Theodore C. "Ted" Sorensen, a lawyer from Lincoln, Neb.

Kennedy's energetic diction, his tone of voice, the simple, measured language of his speeches snapped overhead like a banner in a fresh breeze. It was Sorensen's job to create that banner. He first joined the staff of the newly elected Sen. Kennedy in 1953, and quickly earned a position of trust and responsibility that lasted for the rest of JFK's life. Much of Kennedy's legacy flowed through Sorensen's pen and into the hearts of all Americans.

In private conversation, Ted Sorensen is modest and soft-spoken. Listeners around his lunch table lean forward to catch his words as he banters about the current political scene. At the lectern, he stands tall, still trim at 77, and his hair still dark. Though his eyesight is failing and his voice is quiet, it carries vigorously and with a barbed political point.

"Don't worry about the fact that I can't see . . . I have more vision than the President of the United States."

He greets us as colleagues and proceeds to entertain us with stories from his true peers, the presidential speechwriters of prior administrations. Under the leadership of William Safire, they have formed the Judson T. Welliver society, named for President "Silent Cal" Coolidge's speechwriter, the first of his trade. This group meets periodically at Safire's house to commiserate and wrangle, aiming jibes at one another across the aisle. A few years ago, Peggy Noonan, speechwriter for the Reagan administration, did not show up for a meeting. It seems she had a new book out, Sorensen said.

"So when it came my turn I told them I was sorry Peggy was not there, that rumors that I had helped ghostwrite her book were untrue . . . and then I shook my finger at them and said 'Listen to me carefully. I did not have contextual relations with that woman!'"

He spoke with pride of being a speechwriter and urged us not to permit anyone to refer to us as "just a speechwriter."

"Bear in mind that Alexander Hamilton was a speech-writer for George Washington; Seneca was a speech-writer for Nero; Winston Churchill wrote at least one speech for the King of England. At least he was King until the speech was over."

"Now, if you'll all promise not to violate my copyright, I'll share with you the secrets of speechwriting," Sorensen continued. (Readers are hereby cautioned that the future use of any of his remarks must be accompanied by attribution to Theodore C. Sorensen.) "Speech-writing really comes down to four words and five lines. The four words: brevity, levity, charity and clarity.

Then the five lines are: Outline absolutely indispensable, always the best place to start. No. 2: Headline. What do you want the headline to be? Third: Frontline. What's the most important point, what do you move up to the front? Fourth: Sideline. Put in a quotation from a poem, an allusion to history, a bit of eloquence or precedence from the past. Finally: The "bottom line." What is your conclusion?"

Everyone at my table took notes. Sorensen moved on.

"Humor is extremely valuable to warm up an audience, and sometimes to make a point, but it's not totally without risk. In my very first year, working for Senator John F. Kennedy, I gave him a line which he used. One of our fellow Senators was a very rich Rhode Island nonagenarian, Theodore Francis Green . . . and Kennedy, late for a speech at one of the hotels in Washington, began, at my suggestion, saying to the audience, 'Well, I'm sorry to be late, but fortunately I had a very good cab driver; he got me here in a hurry. I was going to give him a big tip and tell him to vote Democratic, but then I remembered a good idea that Senator Green gave me. I gave him a small tip and told him to vote Republican.' It got a good laugh. Unfortunately, the AP reported the joke as though it was actual fact, and Kennedy heard from every cab driver in Massachusetts."

Sorensen's last tip on speechwriting before opening the floor for questions was to "keep the speech and the speaker together." He then told of an incident when Senator Kennedy was scheduled to speak in Knoxville on the topic of the TVA. Arriving at the airport, the Senator was whisked away in a limousine while Sorensen rode in another car with the staff. "The driver turned on the radio," said Sorensen, "and we hear 'Now from TVA, our speaker for today, John F. Kennedy.' And I've got the speech in my pocket. I said, 'We'll probably want to stay tuned here ...' It was amazing what that man knew about TVA ... after that, he kept the speech in his pocket."

In answer to a question from the floor on writing a great speech, he replied, "A speech is made great, not from the words used, but from the ideas conveyed. If the ideas, principles and values and substance of the speech are great, then it's going to be a great speech, even if the words are pedestrian. The words can be soaring, beautiful and eloquent but if the ideas are flat, empty or mean, it's not a great speech."

Asked about the famous "Ich bin ein Berliner" speech, when did he discover that the local German idiom translated the phrase to mean "I am a jelly donut?" Sorensen responded that his office quickly received that news. "My only recovery was when, two . . . no, three years later, when the USIA sent me on a speaking tour to Germany. I went to the University of Hamburg and explained to them why the President couldn't possibly come there and say "Ich bin ein Hamburger." At which point some wag in the group chimed in "or Frankfurt!"

There were questions about working with JFK, of course, but Sorensen joked about the need for security clearances and declined to answer with a simple, "Ask not."

The phrase presidential speechwriters use when they are asked to inspire an audience is "reaching for the marble." It is a rare and gratifying experience to be in the room and hear the thoughts of one whose words achieved a place on marble walls across America. He is his own best answer to the words from Kennedy's inaugural speech: "Ask not what your country can do for you; ask rather, what you can do for your country."

## About the Author

Mike Landrum is a speaker's coach, speechwriter and actor. He has worked on and off Broadway, had leading roles on daytime TV dramas, and been a spokesman for dozens of corporations and products on national television. As a coach and trainer, Landrum helps top executives with their presentation skills, and as a member of the faculty for Communispond he conducts workshops for mid-level executives and managers. In 2007 Mr. Landrum was awarded the Cicero Speechwriting Award given by the publishers of *The Executive Speaker* and *Vital Speeches of the Day*.

As a speaker, Mike Landrum is available to address audiences of any size on topics of communication, leadership and expanding the spirit. He is the president of his Unitarian Universalist Congregation and is a regular leader at Sunday services.

In addition to monthly issues of the e-zine The Passionate Speaker, Landrum has written articles on public speaking in such publications as The Toastmaster magazine, The Executive Speaker, and Presentations Magazine. Landrum has also written plays, short stories and advertising copy.

He lives in the Hudson Valley, fifty miles north of New York City with his wife, Peggy, a potter, ceramic artist and teacher, and their daughter Elizabeth, 14, a freshman in high school.  To learn more about Mike Landrum and the services he offers, log on to his web site: www.CoachMike.com.

# Index

Printed in the United States
146369LV00003BA/1/P

9 781598 587326